Thanks for
support in buying
my book. Enjoy.

Brenda.

Veronica
Lots of Love June.
Sept. 2011.

Lollipops, Bubblegum, Death and Lies

A young life scarred by a culture of silence

Brenda Fewtrell Brown

AuthorHouse™ UK Ltd.
500 Avebury Boulevard
Central Milton Keynes, MK9 2BE
www.authorhouse.co.uk
Phone: 08001974150

© 2010 Brenda Fewtrell Brown. All rights reserved.

No part of this book may be reproduced, stored in a retrieval system, or transmitted by any means without the written permission of the author.

First published by AuthorHouse 10/26/2010

ISBN: 978-1-4520-5316-5 (sc)

This book is printed on acid-free paper.

DEDICATION

To Susan, the little fair haired beauty who deserved better, and Pamela who was robbed of a sister, but paid the highest compliment to me, 'You are like the big sister I never had'. I love you.

To Ginnette, Karl and Stephen, sometimes you broke my heart, but my love for you will be eternal.

To my husband Michael, the sometime pain in my arse, but I could not have chosen better.

To Bethen, Jordan, Lucy and Millie, the four gifts that God has bestowed upon me. I love you all

Last but not least, to Margaret and Phil, you truly are heaven sent, Your endless listening and none judgemental ways made me open up.

My grateful Thanks to you all. I don't say it often, but I really believe that I have won the Lottery of life.

Contents

Dedication		v
Foreword		ix
Introduction		xv
1.	My arrival	1
2.	Learning the rules	15
3.	Brotherly Love	20
4.	Sexual Progression	33
5.	A young life ends, a young life blamed	42
6.	Newspapers and Lies	52
7.	No opportunity to say goodbye	60
8.	Madness all around	69
9.	Lollipops, bubblegum, and first love	74
10.	Playground talk	82
11.	Another move, same old sex	90
12.	One mental hospital is the same as another	96
13.	Yet again I'm hurting	103
14.	My first experience of cremation	110
15.	Wage earner	118
16.	Pulling teenagers	127
17.	John finally gets his wish	143

18.	Some closures	148
19.	A new perspective on life	167
20.	Mr and Mrs	175
21.	Empty handed, broken hearted	187
22.	Rampant rabbits to family life	202
23.	Same old, same old	219
24.	New home, new life.	232
25.	A new life starts, and another life ends.	247
26.	Owning our own property	269
27.	Back to school!	282
28.	Saying goodbye yet again	294
29.	Mobile !!	303
30.	Help!!	314
31.	Learning to live with it	330
32.	Learning to talk about it	338
33.	Bleak times, yet more revelations	350
34.	The future	363

Foreword

When I first decided to write my memoirs, it was to be a light hearted affair, meant only to be read by my own family. I knew that my daughter, Ginnette, would have kept a copy of the story as a document to be passed down to her family, as it would give an historical insight into the pop groups, bands and music of the time, the make up that was worn, and the fashions that were worn, etc.

It was never intended originally, to include details of the sexual abuse I suffered at the hands of my older brother, as I did not want to remind myself of the shame that I felt, and because I blamed myself for his actions over me. I was a 'big' girl in build, but, my mind was still that of a child, I was very naïve, and had little understanding of 'adult games'. I was not going to give a candid, explicit account of what had passed between John and myself, so the original format of my book was to just touch on the abuse, but to keep the reader guessing. John was after all my big brother, and I felt that I still had to protect him, and myself, by not allowing anyone to be judgemental of our actions.

I had also made a conscious decision, when first writing my story, that I would not burden it with too many names of people who were not relevant to my anguish, be they relatives, colleagues, in-laws, or people in authority. I did not feel that it would be of any benefit to what I was trying to say about my past, and coincidentally, it also meant that problem of 'some names changed to protect the identity', did not have to be wrestled with when the time came to publish.

For very similar reasons I have found it necessary to omit many of the places, events, and holidays, etc. that took place over the intervening years. It would take almost another book to write about them all, despite the weird and wonderful memories they contain!.

Although I came from a large family, with six siblings in all, things were, I feel, often brushed under the carpet, or a 'bury your head in the sand and the problem will go away' attitude prevailed. But as I found out, to my cost many years later, that is a load of rubbish, as when the carpet wears thin, the troubles are still there, and when the storm blows away the sand, the problems become all to visible. However, despite all of the vulnerable, and hard to understand times that I encountered, it never once occurred to me to rebel, attention seek, take drugs or turn to drink. I was passionately loyal to my family, never wishing to hurt any one of them, mentally or physically, so I had to develop a strong survival strategy,...Tomorrow is another day, just keep going!.

Even when I met Michael, who was to become my future husband and father to our children, I ploughed all my efforts into becoming the best friend he had ever had, a loyal wife, and his lover. The same is to be said of Michael, and I had met my soul mate. Then when the children came along, one by one, I took the task of being a mother very seriously, maybe a little too seriously, and as with any new mother, I made all my mistakes with my first child. Having said that, and despite the trials and tribulations that accompany parenthood, all of my children, and grand-children make me proud of them, in many different ways.

So, I have come a long way from those early days when I thought I was going mad, and could not cope with even answering a phone call, or going out to do the simple task of shopping for the essentials, and now there are two ways that I can view my reasons for eventually asking for the help that I obviously needed, via the mental health services. The first being the anger that I felt toward those two people who in recent years, unthinkingly, not knowing what I had suffered in my early years, decided that, 1) I was to blame for the car accident, and so decided to unnecessarily take me to court, and, 2) The parent who somehow blamed me for acting on instructions of senior management, and then also threatened me with court. I <u>could</u> still look back at it with anger, or I could look at it from another point of view,...that both of these men, unwittingly, forced me to seek the help that I had obviously needed for many years previously..

The transcript from the Coroners Court has now confirmed most of the events as I remember them. Although Bob Ward declined to give evidence and John Hathaway lied, I'll never know, without seeing the High Court transcripts, if either was eventually prosecuted for perjury, or for tampering with evidence, or something similar. However, it would mean that I could have gone to the High court merely as a prosecution witness, and not as some kind of suspect, which is how my nine year old mind perceived it to be. If that is true, it might well have been a case of The Crown v Ward, or The Crown v Hathaway, or even Woodford, which of course would mean that I might not even be allowed to see the transcripts, even if they do exist now, and that my quest for justice on Susan's behalf may never be complete. Nevertheless, I am still pleased that I have managed to obtain those very important Coroners Court transcripts after all these years, and to have even travelled this far on my own journey.

As to my reasons for ultimately deciding to publish my story, I originally wanted some justice for Susan, but, as Jane, my psychiatric nurse told me, and quite rightly, I would never get that justice for Susan, but I will hopefully gain some justice for myself by writing it all down, and telling my story in it's agonising entirety....So that is exactly what I have done, no holds barred!.

Introduction

My father was born in 1906 in Birmingham, my mother was born in 1913 in Blackpool, and she was brought to Birmingham in 1920. When my father met my mother, she was a sixteen year old girl, and he was twenty three years old. At the age of seventeen, my mother married my father, she had been a naughty girl, and yes, she was pregnant by four months at the time. She had married above her station, and he had married beneath his, or so I was told many times by my mother. 'The sun shines out of their arses', she told me many times, but I loved my aunts and uncles on my father's side and spent some memorable times with them.

I was the last of my parents six surviving children, although they'd had nine altogether. Stan, my oldest brother, was the first result of my fathers fumble with my mother, followed closely by Sylvia,(known to all the family as Elwyne), then Doreen, Gordon, Jean, Maureen, Barbara, John, and then me.

All families have skeletons in the cupboard, and ours was no exception. I have heard some juicy little titbits, but I can't get to the bottom of any of it, and neither can Doreen or Jean.

Apparently Gordon died at the age of three months, and I have in my possession his funeral arrangement paperwork, but of course, that does not tell me the cause of death. On his black edged remembrance card is a verse,

> An Angel took my child away
> yet I shall not repine,
> since Jesus in his bosom
> wears the flower that once was mine.

Maureen also died in infancy, but the only document I have of that is a small card, written out in fading pencil, telling of a plot number. It is so indistinguishable, that even if I wanted to find her grave, I'd have nothing to go on.

As for Barbara, well, the story goes that my mother was taken into hospital, and Doreen and Jean remember there being 'talk' about Mum going in to have a baby. They remember

Mum going into, and coming home from the hospital, but 'the baby' never materialized. However, one of my aunts, who only had one child, a son, suddenly had a little girl...a baby girl living with them, and her name was Barbara. Apparently, my mother, never talked about 'the baby' to anyone, so, I certainly, can't comment further on that score. I do know, that in times gone by, if a family was poor and had very little means to help the child survive, or the family was already too large to cope with, then it was not uncommon for the child to be 'given away' to someone who could offer them a better life.

My mother was a grafter, taking on any job she could get, from working on the buses, canteen work, piecework, you name it, she'd already had a go at it. I think that her 'gob' got her into trouble sometimes, and that would explain why she'd had so many jobs. She lost one job working for the bus company, (as I was told), because of this. She was a conductress on the Aston run, when a brewery company manager or director boarded the bus, and when Mum asked him what fare he wanted, the reply came back 'tuppence halfpenny'. According to Mum, 'there was no please, nor thank you, no kiss my arse, nothing'. She turned the handle of the ticket dispenser to produce the ticket then punched it, but apparently, the punch did not make the usual ringing tone. As Mum thanked him for his fare and went to walk away, he grabbed her arm, threw the ticket back at her, and made a remark that the ticket machine did not ring. Mum looked down at his hand holding her arm, shook him off, and said 'What do you expect for tuppence halfpenny!.....Bloody Westminster Chimes?'.

She was not one to let anyone get the better of her, and she wouldn't think twice about putting someone in their place. I was with her once when someone had pushed in front of her as she was queuing up for some fruit. This man literally felt the weight of Mum's wrath. She asked him if he thought that she was standing there for the good of her health, and he retorted that she should have been quicker with her purchase. Replying was the wrong thing to do!!.......Mum got her finger, then flicked his lips hard, and told him not to give her any of his cheek, 'jumped up little bastard!'. I was so embarrassed, and he was equally stunned.

Dad was the one who laid down the law, though Mum was the one who dished out the punishment, usually a smack across the face or legs. If I dared to answer back, then she would tell me to put my tongue out so that she could see where all this rudeness was coming from. As I did so, my tongue protruding between my teeth, Mum's hand would swiftly smack me under the chin, and I would bite my tongue!!.

We all had jobs to do round the house, no matter how menial, but Dad would always find something negative to say after our efforts. After we had dusted, he would just have to reach to the highest place where we kids could not reach, and run his finger along an edge, leaving the dust remnants on his finger. 'If a job's worth doing, it's worth doing well', he would say, 'get the duster, stand on a chair and get rid of it'. The old saying, a place for everything and everything in its place, was his key word.

By the time I was born, Dad had mellowed. There is a standing joke between Doreen and myself, if she introduces me to anyone, (which is not often now because she lives in Canada), she will always say, 'this is my baby sister, the brat of the family'. Anyway, big family or not, I'm sure that although we tired Mum out, she loved us all.

My brother John was, without a doubt Mum's favourite. I think this came about because when he was eight years old, he had gone to the 'old rec', (an open area of ground) just down the road from where we lived. The story that I was told is, that as John was playing he was approached by a man, John had gone off with him and had been sexually assaulted by him, and I have always thought this might have contributed to what John put me through in later years.

Mum held a grudge, so if anyone crossed her, then she would fall out with them, and it was Elwyne who she fell out with on a regular basis. Later on in life when I met my now husband, Michael, he didn't even know I had another sister who lived not too far from us. I had been going out with him for eight or nine months before he eventually met her!.

I loved being part of a big family, but from the age of four years old, my family was dwindling down. I liked being an Aunty at the age of four, even though I didn't really understand what an aunty was. I was just told that Elwyne had given birth to a baby, whom she named Susan, and that made me an aunty to her child. I did not know then, that I would play a part in that child's death when she was only five years old, and I was just nine years old. I didn't know then that my Brother, John would cause so much trouble and heartache for my Mum and Dad and put them through hell. I didn't know back then how he would sexually abuse me, and I certainly didn't know, back then, that the secrets I vowed to hold close to my heart would rear their ugly heads in my adult life, as I had always believed that I was mentally strong enough to not allow it to ever happen. People often say, 'children are resilient', but what a cruel joke that can be, as they can't realize that problems often have a habit of catching up with you later in life, especially when you least expect it!.

The fact is, I was **left** to believe that at nine years old, I was somehow responsible for the accident, but this could have been put to rest by my family talking about it back then, however painful it would have been, instead of which **my belief** of my guilt haunted and influenced the rest of my adult life. I can also now see that perhaps my lifelong attempts to hurt no-ones feelings if I could help it, and not to make a fuss about my own problems, have left their own mental scars. My husband, Michael, will often refer to these problems as, 'Being wounded by silence', and that may well describe how I was left feeling for all those intervening years.

One thing is for sure, that If I could turn

back the clock to 1959, and change that day from 10th August, believe me, I would, ... Susan would still be here, and I would not have had my life riddled with guilt.

Chapter 1

MY ARRIVAL

So where does one begin when wanting to tell their own story?. Well, I suppose, at the beginning.

My entrance into the world was 23rd April, 1950. Nothing unusual or spectacular about that, except that my mother did not know that she was actually pregnant with me. She had been having heavy periods, and was diagnosed with a 'growth'. Perhaps these days the word 'growth' might be described as a tumour. My mothers operation was to take place at Dudley Road hospital in Birmingham, on 23rd April, and was to be performed by a Mr Wentworth-Taylor. It was only when she was under the anaesthetic and the tumour was being removed, that <u>my</u> presence was detected, as I was lying behind the tumour, so I was dubbed the 'Miracle' baby by the staff at the hospital.

Mum was by then 37 years old ,and my Dad was 44 years old. They had already had eight children, three of whom had died in infancy. However, according to my older sisters, if my Mum was in shock, my Dad felt as though he was ready for castration, after all Mum had only gone in for the removal of a 'growth' !. There was however, no denying that I was here to stay. Poor bugger, I had no pram, no clothes, no cot, but I did have three older sisters and two older brothers. Dad could hardly believe that he was to start the parenting process all over again, as the oldest of his children was Stan, who at eighteen years old was serving in the merchant navy. Then Elwyne was sixteen years old, Doreen who was fourteen years old, Jean at eleven years old, and John who was seven years old.

Just before I was due to come home from the hospital, Dad gave my eldest sister a £5 note and told her to go and buy me some clothes and nappies, no luxuries then, just the basics. Elwyne brought home a layette, and apparently the knitted trousers were so big for me, that Mum was also able to put my arms inside and tie the laces round my neck,...and I am sure as I got older she wished she could have done that to me many a time!!. As for a cot to sleep in, well a drawer was big enough!.

I was brought home to 71 Alexandra Street, Ladywood. As you can imagine I was spoilt, but not to the degree of later showing any disrespect to either my parents or siblings. I wouldn't have dared, and anyway my in-built personality rendered me incapable of such acts. I was a 'happy go lucky' child, though all that changed when I reached eight years old, and by nine years old my world started to fall apart.

The house we lived in was old, a terraced house with no bathroom, and an outside toilet, the 'Loo', which also accommodated a galvanised tin bath that hung on the wall. We recycled, even in those days, and my job was to tear up the newspaper and thread it onto string to allow the user of the throne to wipe their 'bits'. It didn't matter which newspaper you used, it was still rough on your delicate parts!. At night, no one ventured to the outside loo, instead we had an enamel 'guzunder', or, if you wanted to be posh, a chamber pot, one to each bedroom. It was very primitive by today's standard, and when John used it, it sounded like frozen peas (pardon the pun) hitting a pan. I can feel the coldness on my rear end now, just thinking about it!!. Mum's task would be to traipse to the outside loo in the morning and empty the 'slops'... Ooh nice!

The tin bath would be brought in from the loo on a Friday night and mum would fill it with copious amounts of water that she had boiled in a pan on the old gas stove. The bath would be placed in front of a roaring fire that had been lit earlier that day, using the method of placing a piece of newspaper over the grate recess to 'draw' the flames. Many times we would hear choice language issue forth from Mums mouth as the paper caught fire, and she would shake the paper to try and put the flame out, but this action only fanned the flames more, so she would hastily throw the paper onto the fire, cursing as she did so. I learnt many a new word whilst watching my Mum perform this act!

I loved to watch the flames dance around in the grate and cast their flickering shadows on the wall. I loved it when Mum or my sisters would get out the three pronged extendible fork, place a piece of bread onto the end, then extend the fork, and hold the bread next to the fire to cook, before turning it over to cook the other side giving us hot toast. Mum would spread beef dripping onto the toast, then adding a little salt, and we would munch away blissfully until our tummies were full.

The one thing that that I hated, even back then, was the flypapers that were hanging around the house. In the summer, these brown sticky papers hung like ringlets from the ceiling, with flies trapped by their backs, wings, or bellies, still wriggling their legs to get free. Sometimes the dead flies would be stuck there, motionless, for what seemed like weeks on end......yuk!!

In winter time, we would get ready for the events of Christmas. Mum would encourage me to write to Father Christmas and ask him for the things that I would like. These would be things like a walkie talkie doll, tin cars and tanks, a new 'friction' aeroplane, a wind up tin record player to play my 'Sylvester and tweety pie' record on, and sweets, lots of them!. Once the letter had been written, Mum would get me to 'post' it up the chimney whilst the fire was still burning in the grate. (Dangerous I know, but I was supervised!!). I would then run out of the house to face the sky and watch for my letter to turn into bright orange embers as it left the chimney and wend it's way to Santa.

The excitement mounted even more when Mum took me to see the 'real' Santa at Lewis's department store in Birmingham. Uncle Holly, his assistant would be there to greet us, and we would follow a magical trail until we got to Santa. I would sit on his lap and tell him what I would like for Christmas, a photograph was then taken, and I was given a ticket to take to a window that was marked, age appropriately. I would give the ticket to the lady at the window, and she in turn would hand over a tissue paper wrapped parcel, just a little 'taster' of what was to come. In those days, any thoughts of Santa perhaps being a pervert who liked a quick fiddle with a child just didn't enter your head, and people trusted the person who was employed to do the job of playing Santa. It is a worry though, that perhaps the stringent guide lines of today were not in place, as I don't suppose for one minute that these people were ever 'police checked'.

I loved Christmas, not only for the 'goodies', but it was usual for all of us to be together, Stan, Elwyne, Doreen Jean, John, me and Mum and Dad. Mum would have a bottle of sherry on the go as she prepared the Christmas dinner, and Dad would have his bottle of whisky. Stan would have brought home some fruits from his visits abroad, and I would be content to sit on the floor, playing with my new toys, or colouring in a book with the colourful new crayons that 'Santa' had left for me.

From early on in my life, whilst my older brother was in the navy, my sisters shared the 'attic' bedroom, and I shared a bedroom with my brother John, who was seven years older than me. Mum and Dad had the bedroom opposite us. The accommodation was not ideal, but the best was made of the situation. John and I had separate beds, but I still shared mine!. This was not with family or friends though, this was with little red mites, known as bed bugs!. Dad would often throw back the bed clothes and these little buggers would scurry away, he would get rid of them and assure me that the bed was now all mine,... well, until the next night, at least !.

Like all children, I was afraid of the 'bogey man' in the dark. When I was put to bed I would want the door open and the landing light on. I was made to choose though, it was either the light on and the door closed, or the door open and the light off. I always went for the light on and the door closed, as the gaps in the door allowed chinks of light to enter our room. Before settling down, my Mum would sit on the edge of the bed, and we would say prayers together...

> There are four corners at my bed
> There four Angels stand
> There's one to watch, one to pray
> and two to carry my soul away.
> Amen.

> OR
> Now I lay me down to sleep,
> I pray the Lord my soul to keep,
> but if I die before I wake
> I pray the Lord my soul to take.
> Amen.

Then she would kiss me goodnight, and if it was cold I would have my Dad's big overcoat on top of the blankets to help keep me even warmer. However, on the coldest of winter nights, the ice would creep over, under, and in through the gaps of the window, leaving wonderful ice patterns on the inside of the panes of glass, and there were many times on those winter mornings that I would wake up with a 'mist' coming forth from my mouth.

When it was too cold to play out, John and I would get a blanket off the bed, tie both ends, and position it at the top of the stairs. I would climb in first and hold on to the knot, John would climb in after me, his legs either side of my hips, and, with a push we would bump down the 'rapids', laughing and giggling, and all the time our backs hurting with each thud of each uncarpeted step, but that didn't ever deter us from playing this game again many times. Although John and I would play together in the house, it was a different matter when we were outside, as he would go off with his friends, but I never did cry after him to let me tag along. My games were played with the other girls in the street. We would draw numbers 1-10, on the pavement, and play hop scotch, or we would get one of the bigger boys to loop a rope over the 'arms' of a lamp post, and cradling our bums on the rope, propel ourselves round and round the lamp post.

The one thing that was always guaranteed to interrupt our play was the 'call' of the rag and bone man. He would pull a cart behind him shouting 'any old rags', and we would rush home to pillage Mum's 'rag bag', and bring out items for him to survey. If he wanted them, then our reward would be either a half dead goldfish, a half dead chick, or a toy bird on a piece of string attached to a stick. Holding the stick in your hand, the wind would 'catch' the bird and it would tweet and flutter, and if you ran with it, the faster and louder the tweet became.

If our house was full to bursting when Stan came home from the navy, it was even more so when Elwyne, at the age of twenty, met and eventually married Fred Beasley, and they moved into our house too. At the age of four years old, I think I saw this as having another Mum and Dad, because I would quite often end up in the same bed as them!. These were the days when a child climbing into bed with their older sister was not frowned upon, however, privacy was still respected, and Mum would often call me down stairs so that Elwyne and Fred had some time to themselves. Even so, it wasn't long before they moved out, as Birmingham council soon found a place for them to live in Nechells.

In September,1955, I started my school life at Saint John's school, in Ladywood. Mum took me on the first day, and as she left me there, I tried to be brave, holding back the tears as she kissed me good bye, no doubt with instructions to be good, and that was it. I was left to fend for myself, left to the mercy of people that I did not know, and I feared that I would never see her again!. She did come back for me, of course, otherwise I would not be here now!. I do not ever remember her taking me to school again, as from then on a neighbour took me to, and collected me from school, and by the age of six, I was taking myself to and from school. Mum was working nights and didn't have time for the 'trivialities' of getting me to school, as she needed to get her head down for a sleep. When I walked through the door after school, my Mum would be asleep in a chair by the fire, I would wake her up, and that was her cue to prepare the tea, then as my Dad walked in from his work, Mum walked out to go to hers.

I had only been at school for a few weeks, and I was having trouble seeing the blackboard. Mum was called in to speak to the teacher, and the next thing I knew, I was sitting in a chair at the opticians, where he put a large black lens less frame onto the bridge of my nose, and I remember saying that I didn't like these glasses and didn't want to wear them, as they were much too big and far too heavy on my nose. He explained that he was going to help me to see better than I could now, and placed different lenses into the frame then asked me to tell him if it was better or worse with the lenses in. I don't know if I ever had the right lenses because

I just answered yes or no. There you are, I started to wear glasses and gained myself a new name...four eyes!. I didn't like this name of course, but being the shy, timid child that I was, I never thought to call names back.

One evening, when Mum took Doreen, Jean and John to the cinema, I was left with Dad, and as a treat, I was allowed to sleep in the attic in my big sister's bed. Dad put me to bed, but I wasn't ready to sleep, and as Dad closed the bedroom door, I got out of bed and I began to 'pretend' that I was chasing 'red' Indians, with Roy Rogers and his horse 'Trigger', who at that time were very popular cinema heroes. Those Indians were hiding behind rocks, and Roy Rogers and I had to climb up onto the rocks to get to them. There was a metal bar running the length of the bedroom window, and my imagination was on a roll. I had to get to the top of those 'rocks', so, with my hands placed firmly on the bar, I put both of my feet on the window pane, and started to climb the window. I had not anticipated the 'avalanche', however, and my left foot went straight through the pane of glass, sending shards of glass crashing to the floor below, bugger!....I was for it now, so I shot back into bed and covered myself with the sheet and blankets, blood pouring from the gash in my ankle. My Dad had heard the glass break, and I could hear him running up the stairs, so I closed my eyes, mimicking sleep, but he noticed the window minus the pane of glass, and the blood running down the wall. He suddenly pulled back the bed clothes, and the sheet was no longer white, but a dark crimson colour. He was cursing, then he asked me, 'What the bloody hell have you done?'. He scooped me into his arms and took me down stairs, then very hygienically, he sat me on the table in the living room and told me not to move. He disappeared into the kitchen from where I could hear water running, and on his return he was carrying a bowl of water and a towel. A neighbour had heard the commotion and asked Dad if he needed any help, so he asked her to phone for an ambulance. As Dad sponged my ankle he was calling me a 'silly, silly girl', and I watched as the water in the bowl turned to bright red as he rinsed out the towel. When the ambulance arrived, and Dad carried me into it, people had gathered around to see what was going on, then the doors were closed and we were on our way to Dudley Road hospital. Once there I was given five stitches in my ankle, and Dad was told that I was lucky, if the gash had extended half an inch more, I would have cut the guide in my ankle.

When we got home, Mum, Doreen, Jean and John were already there, as apparently, a notice had been flashed across the cinema screen, asking them to come back home. I'd had a very lucky escape, and I was still allowed to sleep in the attic bedroom with my big sisters. It made me feel really special being allowed to sleep in with my sisters, and I loved them in my own little way.

Chapter 2

LEARNING THE RULES

Mum and Dad were strict with all of us, but I suppose being the youngest, I got away with far more than the others. At meal times we were not allowed to talk at the table, and if the plates were brought in full, then they must leave the table empty, as money was tight, and any food not eaten was a waste. One Sunday lunch time, Mum had done the customary roast lamb and vegetables including green cabbage. I loved my food, so this was not a problem to me, but John hated cabbage and refused to eat it, despite being given the good advice to mash it into his potatoes so that he would not be able to taste it. He did not heed the advice given to him, so when we had all finished our lunch, the cabbage remained on John's plate. I was not prepared for what happened next, as he was given a warning to get it eaten, but instead he folded his arms and refused. Mum and Dad got out of their chairs, and Dad grasped John round his forehead, then with his other hand he forced John's mouth open. Mum then put some cabbage on the fork and put it in his mouth, and although John was crying, Dad closed John's mouth shut and forced him to swallow it. I was screaming at them to leave him alone, as they were hurting my brother. That incident left a profound mark on me, and now I would never force anyone to eat something that they did not like, no matter how hard I had worked with the preparation.

Stan was at the end of his leave and so went off on his travels again. Doreen had now met Sam Amos, and both decided that a better life would be had if they emigrated, so in 1955/6, off they went in search of that better life in Canada. I can remember Mum crying, but I could not understand why, as Doreen would be back soon, and with a stick of rock for me!. Anyway, Mum could always get on a bus to go and see her if she got too sad,.. eh?. So, by 1956 the household had gone from nine people down to just five. Then in 1957 Jean also decided she wanted a life of independence, and she too left home. I have since learned from my sisters, that the life I experienced at home was very different from the one that they encountered, and in fact the reason for my older siblings leaving was down to my Mum. Perhaps I never saw the bad, only the good in people, and that's why I never took much notice. I do know that whatever my parents said was law, and woe betide anyone who did not 'Toe the line', no matter how old you were. If you could not abide by the rules, then it was time to leave.

One of the things that I was taught from an early age was, how to keep a secret, which was usually rewarded with sweets or a colouring book. One of the secrets I had to keep was when Mum had a friend call round, this was not a female friend but a male, and his name was 'Nobby' Burton. He would call on Mum, and they would sit in the living room talking, then Mum would hand me a brown sauce sandwich and tell me to go out and play in the back yard. This was probably innocent enough, but as he was leaving he would tap the side of his nose and say to me, 'not a word to your Dad', then he would give me some sweets and he would leave. I didn't understand the meaning of his action of the nose tapping, and Mum would just tell me that he was a friend of Dads. I never saw them 'doing' anything, but as I have become older I do wonder whether he was Dads friend or Mums 'friend'. I either 'forgot' that he had been round to see Mum, or I could be trusted, through the 'carrot dangling' rewards to keep 'shtum', and as far as I know, I never did breath a word to my Dad.

With just Mum, Dad, John and myself living in Alexandra Street, Mum applied to Birmingham Council for a maisonette in Browning Street, still in Ladywood, but a much more modern place. The council told her that she was already suitably housed, but again, it was the wrong thing to say to my Mum. 'After years of traipsing out to the loo, putting up with bed bugs, damp pouring through every orifice, she wasn't listening to any official who was living in the lap of luxury and took holidays every year, who's wife, no doubt, wore a fur coat and no knickers, and if she did want to go into his home, no doubt it would be all kippers and curtains'. So what did my Mum do?, the sensible thing of course,... she withheld her rent. As was to be expected, she was taken to court for none payment of rent, but Mum had been smart, she'd never been tempted to spend what she'd not paid in rent, and so produced the correct amount of owed rent to the court, and also gained the opportunity to put her side of the case to the court. I don't know how she did it, but a few weeks later we moved to Browning street!.

Chapter 3

BROTHERLY LOVE

The maisonette was so much lighter and cleaner than the house in Alexandra Street, and unlike the old house, had electric fires attached to the walls, posh 'French' windows that lead onto a small patio area, two reception rooms, three light and airy bedrooms, a bathroom with wash basin and toilet, and best of all was a downstairs, inside 'loo'. This was bliss, and our idea of 'keeping up with the Jones's', was to disregard the torn up newspaper loo wipes, and replace it with proper 'tracing paper' loo roll instead, you know, the slippery sort that often gets left behind, so to speak, and crinkled loudly when the user was trying to be quiet and discreet!

It was in this downstairs loo that I tried my first cigarette, as quite wrongly, I had sneaked into Mum's handbag, and taken one out of it's

Lollipops, Bubblegum, Death and Lies

resting place whilst Mum was preparing tea for us. I hid the contraband in my knickers, being careful not to sit down, then I found Mum's matches on the table, took one match out. With my heart pounding, I boldly walked past Mum and into the loo. I opened the small window, fished out the cigarette and put it between my lips, then I struck the match down the loo wall, leaving a thin red stripe in its wake. Holding the cigarette in place I put the lighted match to the cigarette and 'puffed'. I didn't inhale, I just blew the smoke straight out of my mouth. and finished the whole lot, then threw the cigarette butt down the loo and flushed the chain. Bugger!, the stub came back up as if to mock me!, 'now you're for it'. If Mum found out, then she would have given me a walloping, so I tried to get rid of it again. But no, it was here to stay, so there was nothing else for it, I put my hand down the loo and grabbed the soggy, saturated stub and threw it out of the window. When I opened the toilet door, and peeped out to see if Mum was there, I was in luck, she had gone into the lounge, so I went upstairs and into my bedroom, but Mum shouted me down,....God!...she knew!...she knew I had just had a fag!. She didn't scold me for stealing the cigarette, so God only knows what was going through her mind, no, I was told off for leaving that red tell tale stripe on the loo wall!. She just added, 'next time you'll smoke the whole packet until you're sick'. Nothing more was said, there were no wise words such as, 'cigarettes are bad for you', or, 'you'll never have any money if you smoke', or even the famous one of 'wait till your Dad gets home'. I'd had a lucky escape, so from then on I left the smoking habit alone until I reached about fifteen years old.

Because St. John's school (my first school) was now much further away from home, I was sent to a different school, and how different this was. St Peter's, a Roman Catholic school, a school where the fear of God was put into you at an early age!. Mum was still working nights, and so with no older siblings, except John for me to come home to, I was left pretty much to get on with it. John, who was by this time 14 years old, was deemed capable enough to look after me and himself for a couple of hours before Dad came home.

I was in the house alone one day, when John and a friend of his walked in. I went into the hallway, and they both stood looking at me, then out of the blue John asked if I wanted sixpence. Of course I did!, so when I answered 'Yes', I was told by John to show his friend my 'fanny', and the six pence would be mine. I was so embarrassed, and remember feeling my cheeks flush, but they laughed and asked me again. They could stick their sixpence up their arses, as far as I was concerned, I knew right from wrong, and I was having none of that. My 'ha'penny' was my own!.

When his friend had gone and we were left alone, John went upstairs, and then he called me up to look at something. When I went up, he was in bed, and I truly don't know how, but I ended up in bed with him. He put his hand in my knickers and started feeling round, and I remember lying there rigid and frightened, then he told me to go. John stayed in bed for awhile, no doubt so that he could have a fumble with himself, and later he got up and told me not to say anything to Mum and Dad, so I didn't, I kept it to myself, and I told no one of my embarrassment or my wrong doing. I was only seven and a half years old, but I was not a small child even then, by the time I was nine I had boobs, and by ten years old I was in the full throes of periods. Who knows, because of my physical appearance but my childlike naivety, was this a 'turn on' for John?. All I know was that I hated what had taken place, and of course I wouldn't tell Mum and Dad, or anyone else. I was seven and a half years old, so how would I know where to begin?, how could I say to my Mum or Dad, 'John has played with my ha'penny'?. I don't suppose I would have been believed anyway, John, was after all, Mum's beloved, ginger haired, brown eyed boy.

I had two close friends, Janet and Agness. Agness went to the same school as me, and we would walk home together along the canal towpath off Broad Street. It was dangerous, although I never saw the dangers then, as they just aren't seen at that age I suppose, but now I would severely chastise my children if they went anywhere near a canal at that age. Agness always seemed to have some money, and on our way home we would stop at a sweet shop and she would buy sweets for both of us. She was always generous, and of course, being a greedy little devil, I never thought to refuse.

Because I was a non-Catholic attending a Catholic school, I was given the ultimatum of either leaving, or changing my religion, and since I had made a few friends there, I begged Mum to let me stay at that school. It meant being baptized into the Roman Catholic faith, going to confession, and making my confirmation. That in itself was a farce, because my Dad claimed to be an atheist, and he would play no part in Mum's decision, so one day I went to the church with Mum and the priest baptized me into the faith.

When it came to making the confirmation, all the little girls were dressed as miniature brides, in white dresses and a veil, rosary beads and bible in hand, and all the boys, in white suits. Me!, Christ, it's a good job that I took no notice, as I was wearing a pink and white flecked short sleeved dress, talk about sticking out like a sore thumb!. In fact the only 'virginal' thing about me that day were my white socks. Once back outside the church, children were being kissed and some were being given gifts, but there were no such niceties for me, and I walked beside Mum straight home, where dinner was prepared. Dad didn't ask how it went, the deed was done, and that was it, I was now a Roman Catholic. In itself that meant very little to me, other than when I made my confession I would have to keep some of the truth close to my heart, and not tell anyone of the wicked things I was doing with John, as by then his advances towards me had escalated.

Like a good Catholic girl, and having the religion forced down my throat at school, I thought that when I got older, I would like to become a nun. However, when I got into the confessional box, I would start with 'Bless me Father for I have sinned, these are my sins,...I have lied, I missed church last Sunday, (that wasn't unusual), I have eaten meat on a Friday', (as if my Mum was going to cook fish just because I was Catholic), and so it went on. I would come out of the confessional armed with my rosary beads, and with instructions to say three 'Our Father's', and ten 'Hail Mary's'. Then, just so that I could get home quickly, and because my friends were more important than my prayers, I would gabble them quickly, almost missing out beads as I did so. I don't think that the Roman Catholic church was quite ready for a nun like me, as after all, how could I take my religion seriously when my Dad would take me to the museum, or to my aunts and uncles, or the railway station on a Sunday. Given the choice of one of those visits or going to church, there was no competition really. The following Monday at school, however, the first question was always the same, 'hands up if you were at Mass yesterday'. My hand lied, because it would always shoot up, and guess what?, I was always found out, and why?, because then the teacher would ask what the service was about,...and I hadn't got a clue!. So I would be sent to the head teachers office and given a lesson on the sacrifices Jesus had made, and did I think he died just so that I could defy his teachings?, defy Gods ten commandments, 'Remember that thou keep holy the Sabbath day'. But then there was another one of the ten. 'Honour thy Father and thy Mother'. I couldn't to say to my Dad, 'I can't come to my Aunts and Uncles today, I have to go to church'....Clout.!!.

Dad worked on a Saturday morning, and Mum would go shopping, leaving John in charge of me. If I woke on time, I would hurry to get dressed and go with her, but I think that I was more of a hindrance than a help.

One of those Saturdays, when Dad was at work and Mum was shopping, I was still in bed when I felt John get into bed with me again. He wasn't rough, he wasn't tender, it was just an action with him. As I felt my pyjama trousers being pushed down, I told him 'no!, leave me alone', but he asked me to hold his 'cock', nothing more, then he would leave me alone. He threw the bed clothes back exposing his penis through his flies, and as I held him, he put his hand over mine so that my grip on him was tighter, and he started to move my hand up and down. I felt his penis swell, and I was so worried, repulsed and frightened, my heart was beating faster, what would happen if Mum came home from her shopping trip?, I'd really be for it then!. Suddenly for some reason, he stopped, got out of bed, did up his flies and went down stairs with the usual command, 'don't tell Mum and Dad'. I went into the bath room and washed my hands, then back into the bedroom, closed the door and dressed myself. A short while later I went down stairs as though nothing had happened, and when Mum came home with the shopping she asked John if I had been good, to which he replied that I had, (though I'm surprised he didn't say 'better than good' with what I had just done!). Mum then handed me some sweets, and she was none the wiser as to what had happened to me.

Some Sundays, when Dad would take me out, It gave Mum some time to herself, to prepare the Sunday roast, and catch up with the housework, but the one job Mum never did on a Sunday though, was the washing, I don't know why, but she just never did. Dad would take me to see one of his brothers and their wives, or his sisters and their husbands. We would visit Aunty Dolly and Uncle Albert who lived in the Ridgeway, opposite Witton

Cemetery. Their house was detached, quiet and clean, the clock ticking was the only sound to disturb the quiet amidst the adult talk. Aunty Dolly would make us a cup of tea and bring in a plate of biscuits, the cups and saucers were delicately decorated with flowers, and the plates would match. I would wait to be offered a biscuit off the plate, and then I would rest the biscuit in the saucer until I was ready to eat it, as It made a change from diving into the biscuit packet and dunking it into your 'cuppa' as we did at home!. When we left, Uncle Albert would take out a two shilling piece and place it in my hand. It made me feel so rich and I was always grateful for his generosity.

Aunty May and Uncle Arthur were other relatives we would visit. They lived in Saltley, and like our old house in Alexandra Street, their loo was outside in a block which was shared by the other neighbours. I would hold myself rather than go to the toilet there, because the smell of pooh and pee was sometimes overpowering, as there wasn't always enough water in the bowl to cover the remains of the last person to use it. I got on well with both of their children, though they were slightly older than me and preferred to be in the company of their Mum and Dad rather than be adventurous, so we would sit in the house and play. I must admit that I don't ever recall being offered anything to eat and drink in their household. I do know that we visited Aunty Rene and Uncle Sam, but, sad to say, and in all honesty, I don't remember much about those visits. Their children were about the same ages as Doreen and Jean, my older sisters, so perhaps that is why I don't have any memorable recollections of those visits.

If it was not convenient to visit my aunts and uncles, then Dad would take me to Snow Hill Railway station, where we would spend time watching the different trains coming and going, and waving to the drivers. Steam would permeate this building, with people suddenly appearing and disappearing out of these mists like spectres. The porter would be transporting cases or goods to the rear of the train on his hand pulled trolley cart, then the guard would blow his whistle, and wave a green flag to signal to the driver of the train that all the passengers were aboard, and that it was now safe for him to depart. I would watch as some of the passengers pulled the sash belt which would allow the window to drop, and they would lean out of the window to wave to their friends or loved ones before starting their journey. As the train pulled out of the station there would be a loud hiss, and the train would shunt heavily as the buffers hit each other, then the smell of coal filled the building, and would stay in your nostrils long after the train had left for its destination,... and all of this enjoyment for a 2d platform ticket!!. I really loved those visits, but hasten to add that I did not become a 'train spotter', and I do not wear an anorak !!.

Sometimes, my Dad would take me to the Birmingham Museum and art gallery, and the first thing that always struck me, (not literally!), on entering the museum was the musty smell, and the highly polished banisters. Dad and I would walk up the steps, and in the main foyer was, I think, the fallen Angel, Lucifer. This beautiful sculpture stood high on a plinth, and as a child, when I looked up, it was obvious to me that he must have been very poor because he wore no clothes, so that his 'tackle' was on display for all to see. People would talk in hushed tones, and I would watch people as they stood and scrutinized the paintings by famous artists, their heads tilted, or their hands rubbing their chins, others had a pencil and pad, and were copying the paintings. I am ashamed to say, that I felt this wealth of talent quite boring!. I always found the natural history section far more interesting, and as for the Egyptian section...wow!!. I wanted to know more about the Pharaoh's, their life style, how they built the pyramids, how they were embalmed, and what the hieroglyphics meant. I found the Egyptian section so fascinating that I wanted to spend more time in there, and Dad would answer my persistent questions on Egyptology as best he could, but with everywhere in the museum being so quiet, I was always afraid to raise my voice in excitement for fear of disturbing the silence. All too soon the visit would be over, and we would travel home by bus, back to Mum who was in the usual throes of preparing the Sunday roast. As a child, I always enjoyed those visits, and as an adult I realize how lucky I was to have a parent who took the time to show me these things. I have never found a museum boring since then.

Chapter 4

SEXUAL PROGRESSION

By 1958, the gypsy in Mum surfaced again, and she wanted to move from Ladywood to Kingshurst, a new-ish area on the outskirts of Birmingham. We moved to a ground floor flat, where the area was kept nicely, although the flat was slightly smaller, having only one bathroom complete with toilet and wash basin. We still had three bedrooms, one living room, a kitchen, a little garden, and it boasted a 'veranda' at the front of the house. I was eight years old, and this move meant yet another address for me to remember, this time it was 43, Ash Crescent. Three addresses to remember in eight years, not bad going eh!

I quickly made friends with the other children who lived in the same flats, people like June, Eunice, Pauline and Kenny. We would put on our ball bearing roller skates and skate up and down the road, and If we put oil on the wheels, my word, we could really get a move on!. We would play games like 'Queeny, queeny who's got the bally oh?', L.O.N.D.O.N, and the perennial hopscotch. We could buy sweets from the mobile grocery shop that came down our road, and we would pick daisies off the lawns to make daisy chains. Sometimes we would make birds nests out of the grass that had been freshly mowed, not realizing that these nests would never be occupied, no matter how lovingly they had been made. We would have glass marbles, and make a hole in the soil with the heal of our shoes to play 'holey', a game in which you would have to try and aim your marble into the hole, with the one who got the most marbles into the hole being the winner...and the one who kept all the marbles!.

Again, because of the house move, I had to go to another school, so until Mum became familiar with the area, the only school she found for me to go to was Kingshurst County Junior, where I must have stayed for all of two terms!. Mum soon found out that there was a Catholic school called The Guardian Angels school in Shard End, which was the next area to Kingshurst, and I started my education at that school in Easter 1959. There are a couple of notable things that happened there, but only one worth mentioning here. Every Monday morning we had a spelling test, but the week before I had been ill, and so I did not know, or have time to revise the spellings that had been given out. On the Monday, true to form we had the test, and 'Brains' here only managed to get a measly three out of ten, ...Oops!. So Mr Heskins, the form teacher, called me and two or three other children out to the front of the class room, and humiliated us by saying we were stupid, and that we were to be punished so that we would learn our spellings next time. He used a ruler on the backs of our legs, and even by the time I got home, the weal marks on my legs were still visible. Mum asked me what they were, but although I didn't want to tell her, she soon got it out of me. The next day, she took some time off work, marched me into the Headmasters office and demanded to see Mr Heskins, and said she would not leave his office until she had seen him. When Mr Heskins walked in, Mum picked up a ruler that was on the Headmaster's desk, held it up to his face, and told him that if he ever touched me again, she would 'shove the ruler so far up his arse, he would be spitting numbers out of his mouth for ever', then she grabbed my hand and marched me home for the rest of the day. My God!, I had to go and face him alone the next day!, however, he never touched me again, In fact I don't think he ever talked to me again!.

Mum and Dad were heavy smokers, and one day a salesman knocked the door, which I answered. He asked me, 'Is the lady of the house at home?', but I had no idea what he meant, so I called for Mum. He then asked her if anyone in the house smoked. Well, both Mum and Dad smoked heavily, so Wow!, was this a lucky day for him, and heaven on earth for my Mum. So the salesman went on to explain that he was promoting cigarette machines, and he just happened to have one with him if she wanted to take a look. Mum asked him to come back later that day when my Dad was home, and when the salesman returned, they invited him into the house. The cigarette machine was to be rented, and he would call once a month for the rental, at which time he would also fill the machine with the 'ciggies' that they smoked. Although I can't remember how much this 'coffin nail' machine cost per month, they went ahead with the rental, and he filled the machine with Players Senior Service, and Capstan full strength. It was Mum who smoked the

Capstan full strength, and she was so hooked on them that she would stick a pin in the end of the cigarette, just so that she could get one last puff from it, and she has even been known to burn her lips from smoking too close to the butt.

If that wasn't bad enough, Davenports Brewery used to deliver beer to our house too. It was almost like having your own private 'Pub', with the crate of empty bottles to be left outside our front door on a Friday ready for the fresh delivery on Saturday. Its a shame 'Walkers' or 'Golden Wonder' didn't deliver crisps and nuts, as we'd have had the whole gamut then!.

Although they were having beer delivered, Mum would like the odd drink of whisky and tonic, and some Saturday evenings she would announce to my Dad that she was just 'popping' over to the outdoor at the Toby Jug pub to buy herself a small bottle of whisky and a soda siphon. She would tell me to get my coat on and walk over to the pub with her. It would be an hour or so later that we would return home, but why should it possibly take that long?. Well, it's because she'd meet a man over there, Alec Smith, who she had apparently known for some time, and at the Toby Jug, they would have a drink together, and I would be brought some pop and crisps. They would talk, and I do remember them holding hands, then after an hour or so we would take our leave, at which time he would say to me, 'Not a word to your Dad!'. Bloody hell!, that sounded familiar, the secrecy had started all over again. When we were walking home, Mum would say to me, 'if your Dad asks why has it taken so long, I shall tell him they didn't have the soda siphon at the Toby Jug, so we had to walk to the Mountford pub, I don't want you saying anything....you just let me do the talking'. When we opened the front door, my Dad would say, 'where the bloody hell have you been?', and Mum would tell him exactly what she told me she would say. This only happened three or four times, and I don't think for a minute Dad believed her, but I am just glad that he never put me in the firing line for questioning.

John by now had started work, so I would come home from school to an empty house until Mum got home. John still seized the opportunity to do what he wanted to do to me, and one half term, he feigned illness and stayed off work, then when Mum and Dad had gone to work, he got into the bed with me. Perhaps I should have been stronger and pushed him off, after all I was a big girl physically, but I don't know why, perhaps I felt sorry for him, perhaps I thought that he didn't know right from wrong, perhaps it was just the fact that he was my big brother and that I loved him in my own way. By this time he had progressed to placing his fingers into me and just playing with me, asking me if it was nice, and that I was to hold him. As usual his penis grew, and next he was on top of me pushing his penis between my vulva. I was old enough to realize that babies were put inside the female via the male penis, but I didn't realize that it had to be full penetration, that a woman had to be ovulating, and to ovulate, periods had to be started, and this had not happened to me yet. I also did not know that sperm was to be produced to fertilize the female egg. Once again I felt anxious, I felt worried, I felt dirty, and I told him not to make me pregnant, upon which he told me not to be so stupid, as that wasn't going to happen, but with my lack of knowledge, how could I be sure of that, and how would I even know if I was pregnant?. John buried his head into my neck, and I was still pleading with him to not get me pregnant, when suddenly he stopped and snapped at me, 'It won't happen!'. Then he got up and disappeared out of the bedroom, and I washed and straightened myself out. As usual nothing more was said.

For a while I was safe, because in 1959, whilst in Portugal, Stan had married Maria Du Carmo Elmades, a Portuguese girl, and she was soon coming over to England. Unfortunately, because Stan was not resident in England they did not qualify for a council house, so they moved in with us. From then on, whilst Stan was still in the merchant navy, Marie stayed at home with us, which meant she was always at home when I came in from school, even when Mum and Dad were out. I liked having Marie living with us, it was almost like having the full house that I remembered from my childhood, especially when Stan was home with us too.

In past years, when Mum and Dad had their annual holidays, we wouldn't go away for the whole week, but would take excursions by train to Rhyl or Blackpool every other day. This particular year, in the August, Elwyne and Fred had invited us to their house in Francis Street, Nechells, and by this time Elwyne had two children, both girls, Susan who was five years old, and Pamela who was three years old. When in the past we had spent Christmas with them, going to their house on Christmas Eve, and staying until

Boxing day, we would sleep three in the bed, with me sandwiched between Elwyne and Mum, Dad and Fred sleeping off the effects of the whisky bottle in another room, and Susan and Pamela tucked up in bed in their own bedroom waiting for Santa. To me it was a lovely time, spending precious hours with my big sister, so I was pleased to be going to their house for dinner that August day, but If only I could have seen just a little into the future, my life would have turned out so differently.

Chapter 5

A YOUNG LIFE ENDS, A YOUNG LIFE BLAMED

On the 10th August,1959, Mum, Dad, and I caught the bus from Kingshurst, to Elwyne and Fred's terraced house in Nechells. When we arrived, Susan, Pamela and I went into the back garden, which was really no more than a rubble patch, devoid of any flowers or even a lawn, the soil was dry and dusty, and there was a crumbling wall at the far end of the garden. I soon went back into the house, but Susan and Pamela followed me as they still wanted me to play with them, so we went back into the garden where there was nothing to do, and nothing to play with. Elwyne then suggested that I put Susan and Pamela in the pushchair and take them for a walk round the block, which must have taken me all of ten minutes to do, then I walked back up the alley way at the side of the house and let Susan and Pamela out. I had done as requested by my oldest sister, and now felt that I could go in to the house and listen to the adults talk. Susan and Pamela had followed me into the house again, to where Elwyne was standing by the kitchen sink, potato in one hand and a knife in the other, preparing our dinner. Once again Susan asked me to go into the garden, but this time I objected, I didn't want to go, and so Susan began to cry. Elwyne suggested that I took both girls round the block in their pushchair just one more time, and by the time we got back, our dinner would be ready.

So, I did what most nine year old girls do best,...I whined, I pulled a face, I protested,...I really didn't want to go, or take Sue and Pam out yet again, however, yet again I relented. Sue got in at the top end of the pushchair, and Pamela sat on the raised foot rest with a blanket under her bottom, facing Susan. As it happens, neither girls were wearing safety reigns, so, if there is a God to thank, at least I can thank Him for that. Susan was holding onto the sides of the pushchair, giggling, and once both were settled, I began to push them both back down the alleyway, and at the end of it I turned left onto the street.

When I came to the next corner on the

left, I heard the noise of an engine, or an exhaust somewhere behind me. I must have subconsciously taken in the scene around me, and there were some older children playing opposite me, the houses were casting shadows, and there was a brick wall to my left, again with dry soil and no buildings on it. Still holding onto the pushchair, I turned my head slightly to my right, inching the pushchair next to the brick wall, as there was nowhere else I could go.

The rumbling of the lorry sounded closer, and the next thing I can remember was one of the rear wheels of the lorry mounting the pavement , and the handle of the pushchair being snatched from my hands, as it somehow it became wedged under the rear wheels. I remember feeling puzzled, as the lorry showed no signs of stopping, and I ran towards the rear of the lorry, vainly hoping I could release the handle of the pushchair. I watched in turmoil, as Pamela was thrown out to the left, towards the wall, and I didn't know whether to stop and tend to her, or, though God knows what I could do, to try to help Susan, then I stopped, absolutely rigid and terrified, as if paralysed in my mind as well as my body.

The older children on the opposite side of

the road could hear the commotion and they were shouting a name, 'Mr Ward, Mr Ward !', urging him to stop, as I watched, helpless, not knowing at all what to do. Pamela was crying, I could feel panic waving across me, and I could see that Susan was still clutching the sides of the pushchair, her body bent forward. I could see her face, (and this memory will stay with me until the day I die), this little face, with her blonde hair slightly covering it, was full of fear. Susan was only five years old for Gods sake, what was that all about?. Then the handle of the pushchair crumpled and her little body was thrown to my right, her left, but the wheels kept on moving and Susan disappeared beneath them. That Bastard of a lorry driver just kept on going, unaware(or was he), of what was happening, despite the commotion, despite surely feeling a bump, even the sounds of metal crunching as the pushchair was crushed. I started to run towards Sue, and God knows I was torn between Pam and Sue, but I just knew I had to go to her.

The full horror of what had just taken place hadn't registered in my mind, for in my innocence I tried to pick her up. She was floppy, and her eyes were closed, but I thought, 'she's OK', only because there wasn't much blood, as I recollect. What a joke, what a cruel trick of nature to impose on me and Susan, of course there wouldn't be much blood, would there?, her injuries were internal, due to having been squashed by the two back wheels of the lorry.

All of these events must have happened within two or three minutes, but it seemed to be lasting hours for me. Suddenly, I just knew that I was going to be in trouble, as people were running round, with Elwyne running faster than anyone else. Looking back on it, I think that I must been suffering from some form of shock, or in my child's mind, I just could not absorb the severity of what had happened just moments earlier.

The owner of the nearby garage, who was one of the few in the street to own a car, got Elwyne, Susan and Pamela into his car and sped off to The General Hospital, in Steelhouse lane, in the centre of Birmingham, which is now, ironically, called The Children's hospital, and I remember looking into the car and seeing Elwyne crying, and the look of utter disbelief and despair in her face. I recall looking back at Mum and seeing the tears in her eyes, and my Dad having his arm linked in hers for support. What had just happened must have been so shocking, too awful for

Lollipops, Bubblegum, Death and Lies

words, because there was no telling off, no smacks or hysterics, just sobbing.

The police had been called, and I remember climbing into the rear of the police car, and being flanked by Mum and Dad. We were taken to The General Hospital and shown to the cubical where Elwyne, who had now been joined by Fred, sat with Pamela, but there was no sign of Susan, who had apparently been taken straight to the operating theatre. When a doctor came into the cubical, I was ushered away from any talk, so it was only later that day that I found out that Pam had escaped with cuts and bruises, and although the doctors had fought for three hours to save Susan, their fight, and Susan's, had been in vain. Just a few hours earlier, she was alive and she had been crying for me to play, or to take her out, but now she was gone, and because of me, a family would be torn apart. What followed, for me, was an incomprehensible time, as It meant nothing to me, other than, Susan was dead,...because of me.

How did I feel?, no one ever asked. Frightened and confused, I wanted some one to hold me and tell me that it was going to be alright, but that wasn't going to happen to me, why should anyone be thinking of what

I might be going through?. I couldn't believe that I would not be seeing Susan again, and I thought that tomorrow would be just another day, that it had ended there, at the hospital, that I would be going home and all would soon be well. By the same token, In my nine year old child's mind, I believed that the blame for Susan's death must lie with me, and only me, that I had killed my niece. I thought I would be sent to prison, and yes, these were strong thoughts for a nine year old girl, but I knew right from wrong, and what had happened was wrong, and that people who were guilty of doing wrong, went to prison. The fact that I was only nine years old seemed totally irrelevant in those circumstances!. I had not long been converted into the catholic faith and had learnt of the ten commandments, not particularly in the right order, but there was the one about 'thou shall not kill'. These were the commandments given to Moses by God, and as far as I was concerned, I had broken one of his commandments, and from my teachings at the Catholic school, it was a mortal sin to break any of them, and sinners had to be punished!. Hence my reason for believing that I would be sent to prison.

I was asked a barrage of questions by the police, followed by more from the press. After this was the Coroners court and finally Victoria Law court. As far as I know, the children that had been playing opposite had told the police that it had been Bob Ward's lorry, so he was arrested and taken in for questioning. If I felt unsure and confused on the day Susan had died, then the time for me in the days and weeks after her death was even more confusing and bewildering, as the questions came thick and fast from what seemed to be a multitude of people, all asking me to recount the events of 10th August.

The worst of the questioning came from Barristers at the Victoria Law court. The Victoria Law Court buildings in Birmingham date from 1887-1891, and the main entrance doorway boasts two imposing gothic towers, but although the rear of the court is much plainer, not quite so fancy, it does have a motto, **'Justice giveth everyone his own'**. Justice for who?. There was certainly no justice for Susan, and there never would be for me.

The court, though elaborate, was a dark building, with high ceilings and highly polished rails and seating. There were a lot of people milling about, men in wigs and gowns, ushers calling out names, and people speaking in hushed tones. I sat with Mum and Dad, then when my name was called, I was led into a room where people were sitting, and although I was a big girl, I felt dwarfed by the box that I had to stand in, and by the large desk that the magistrate sat behind. I felt totally alone and confused, worried that I was going to be 'told off', then a book was thrust into my hand...a bible, and I was told to repeat what the man was going to say, **"I swear to tell the truth, the whole truth and nothing but the truth"**. They asked my name, and then I was asked if I knew what truth meant, so I replied, "its not a lie". The same man then asked me to recount the events of 10th August, and at the time I didn't know that Bob Ward was in the courtroom. As I recounted the events of that day, I was questioned, questioned and re-questioned, then at one point there was a recess, and I got talking to one of the children who'd been playing on the opposite side of the road that day. I don't recall now which girl it was, but she told me that, if I was asked, I should tell the jury that the make of the lorry was a Bedford.

Once back in the courtroom, I was asked if I had taken the registration number of the lorry, Christ !...I didn't even know what a registration was, let alone take it, but then I answered that I knew it was a Bedford lorry. Big mistake...I was then asked if I knew the difference between, say, an Austin or a Bedford lorry, (well, of course, would any child of nine?, I don't think so!), so I answered "no", and this horrible man, this barrister, might just as well have smacked me in the face, as it was pointed out that I had lied under oath, that I had sworn on the bible to tell the truth. On and on it went, I had been shot down in flames, belittled in front of so many people, including Bob Ward, and I believed that because of that lie, Bob Ward got away with it. There was no evidence that he was driving, or that it was indeed, his lorry, so the case was thrown out. Hit and run, accidental death, it didn't matter, because Bob Ward was free...case not proven.

Chapter 6

NEWSPAPERS AND LIES

At this point, I need to come forward to 2005. Fred and Elwyne's marriage had long since broken up, and in August 2003 Elwyne had died, with Fred having died two years before Elwyne. For reasons I will go into much later, I went to see Pamela who gave me some newspaper cuttings that Elwyne had kept in her possession, but that I had never seen before, so I include these, verbatim.

Taken from Birmingham Evening Despatch, Tuesday 11th August, 1959
'Widen Death corner' petition for city.
GIRL DIED AS LORRY HIT PRAM.

A five year old Birmingham girl was killed when a lorry smashed her pushchair under it's rear wheels in Francis Street, Ashted.
The dead girl Susan Beasley of 162, Francis Street and her sister Pamela,

aged three, were being taken for a walk by Brenda Fewtrell (9) of Ash Crescent, Kingshurst. The sisters were being pushed along the pavement near their home, when a lorry mounted the footpath and collided with the pushchair. Pamela and Susan were taken to the General Hospital where Susan died. Pamela was discharged after treatment for bruises and cuts.

As Susan's father, Mr Fredrick Beasley sat at home last night nursing Pamela, he said, DEATH TRAP.

"That corner, where the street turns left is a death trap. There are always kiddies playing there, and lorries have to go on the pavement to get round".

Francis Street residents are now being asked to sign a petition pressing the city council to widen the bend where Susan died. Mrs Margaret Ingram who is organising the petition said "it is a very dangerous corner".

Taken from Birmingham Evening Mail Wednesday 19th August, 1959.

GIRL (9) TELLS OF FATAL CRASH.

A 19 year old motor cyclist today told the Birmingham Coroner, Mr G. Billingham, how he chased a lorry after a street accident in which two little sisters were injured, one fatally.

The inquest was on five year old Susan Beasley, of 162 Francis Street, Nechells. Susan and her three year old sister, Pamela were in a pram being pushed in Nechells, by nine year old Brenda Fewtrell, of Kingshurst Estate. The pram was struck and dragged along the pavement. Susan died from her injuries. Pamela was only slightly hurt. Brenda escaped injury.

Mr John Hathaway of 15 Paget Road, Pype Hayes, a mechanic at Bucks Garage, Francis Street, said that after failing to catch the lorry, he saw one which he was certain was the one involved, parked outside a house in Francis Street. On the nearside rear mud guard were several marks of maroon paint and white rubber marks off the pram.

Brenda Fewtrell said she was on the footpath with the pram and close to the wall, "A lorry mounted the footpath and snatched the pram out of my hands" she said.

Taken from Evening Despatch Wednesday 19th August, 1959.

I DIDN'T TELL POLICE THE TRUTH, SAYS INQUEST YOUTH.

A nineteen year old youth told a Birmingham inquest today that he did not tell the truth about a lorry when questioned by a police man.

Earlier four little girls told the jury how

they saw a lorry mount the pavement in Francis Street, Nechells, and collide with a pushchair carrying two small children.

The inquest was on Susan Elaine Beasley, (5), of 162 Francis Street, who died in Birmingham General Hospital a few hours after the accident on August 10th. Susan's three year old sister was also injured. The city coroner, in his opening remarks to the jury, said he understood the evidence would be that a lorry apparently mounted the footpath, and dragged the pushchair and went on without stopping.

Brenda Fewtrell, (9) of 43, Ash Crescent, Kingshurst Estate, Castle Bromwich, said she was taking Susan and Pamela, her nieces along Francis Street in the pushchair. "I was close to the wall" she said. "a lorry came from behind as I was on the corner. It mounted the footpath and snatched the pushchair out of my hands, the pram got smashed and ran over Susan".

Three children who were together on the footpath opposite the corner then gave evidence. They were Diane Wardingly, (14) of 3, Bloomsbury Street, Nechells. Sandra Townsend (11) of 5, Bloomsbury street and Wendy Smith (12) of Francis Street, Nechells.

WE SHOUTED

Each told the Jury how they saw a lorry mount the pavement at the corner and dragged the pushchair along. They said they had seen the lorry before and it was usually driven by Mr Ward. Sandra said, "It was being driven this time by Gary's dad, Mr Woodford. We shouted to Mr. Ward to stop but the lorry carried on". In answer to a juryman, Sandra said Mr Ward was also in the lorry with Mr.Woodford.

John Hathaway (19) of 15 Pagets Road, Pype Hayes, motor mechanic at Bucks Garage said, "I heard a lorry passing which I recognised as being Mr Wards". After he heard screams and had been told what happened, he got on his motor cycle and went after a black lorry. "As I was going round the block I got to the top of Francis Street and saw Mr Wards lorry stationary outside his house. I recognised the two men in the vehicle. Mr Woodford was driving. I did not go down to the vehicle but returned to the garage. A policeman then came down the road with Mr. Ward, and Ward said to me 'was it my vehicle?'. I said 'No'.

TRYING TO HELP.........

The policeman asked me what kind of lorry it was, I told him it was black and I recognised it as an Austin. I was not telling the truth because I didn't think the accident was serious at first, I was trying to help Mr. Ward. I went back into the work shop and Mr Ward followed me. He said 'was it my vehicle?'. I replied 'We'll go and find out'. Mr. Ward, Mr. Woodford and myself went and looked at his lorry. There were maroon paint marks and white rubber marks off the pram on the rear mudguards. I pointed to the marks and said 'There's the proof that it was your vehicle'. After that Mr Ward rubbed off some of the marks with his fingers. I returned to the garage and that evening I went to the police and told them what I have told the court today". said Mr Hathaway.

The policeman did not say he was satisfied with what he had told him about the lorry, said Mr Hathaway. When they were looking at the lorry, Mr. Ward had said that the marks were old ones............

PROCCEDING

GIRL INQUEST IS ADJOURNED;

The Birmingham Coroner (Mr. G. Billington) today adjourned until next Wednesday the inquest on a five year old girl who was killed on Monday when a lorry struck the perambulator in which she was being pushed. The girl, Susan Elaine Beasley, of 162 Francis Street,

Nechells, died in the General Hospital the same day.

Inspector Stanley Evans said that his enquiries were not quite complete.

Susan was in the pram with her three year old sister Pamela, when the lorry, travelling in the same direction struck the perambulator.

LORRY STRUCK PRAM, JURY UNABLE TO SAY WHO WAS DRIVING.

Returning a verdict of 'Death by misadventure' on a five year old girl killed when a lorry mounted the pavement and struck her pram, a Birmingham inquest jury added, "We are satisfied she was ran over by a lorry, but we are unable to say who was driving it at the time".

The inquest was on Susan Elaine Beasley, of 162, Francis Street, Nechells.

The Coroner (Mr. G. Billington) told the jury; "You may think it a disgraceful thing that a child should be killed while on the footpath in broad daylight".

Susan's three year old sister Pamela who was in the pram with her, was slightly injured. Nine year old Brenda Fewtrell of 43, Ash Crescent, Kingshurst Estate, Castle Bromwich, who was pushing the pram on the pavement in Francis Street, was unhurt.

GIRLS EVIDENCE

Three girls standing on the opposite pavement told the coroner that the lorry was usually driven by Sidney James Robert Ward, of 169, Francis Street. The girls Diane Wardingley (aged 14), Sandra Townsend (aged 11) and Wendy Diane Smith said they saw Mr William George Woodford of 171, Francis street, Nechells driving the lorry at the time of the incident.

In an alleged statement read to the court, Mr. Ward said he was driving. **HE DECLINED TO GIVE EVIDENCE IN COURT.**

Mr. Woodford told the coroner he thought the reason the children thought he was driving was because he was seated in the centre of the cab. The children were more likely to recognise him than Mr. Ward because he sold them ice cream.

The Coroner was told that scratches were found on the kerb for 76 feet and the pram was squashed flat.

Chapter 7

No opportunity to say goodbye

One the day of the funeral, I was to stay at home with Marie. I had asked Mum and Dad if I could go, and was told 'best not to', so I played out with my friends as though nothing had happened. Of course I realise now, as an adult, that if I had gone, Fred would probably also have put me in the ground. From that day, 10th August, he hated me, he saw the whole thing as my fault and told me as such. I could not explain how I felt, though I do know that I wanted to go to the funeral, but I couldn't tell you why. Perhaps if I had been allowed to go, I would have accepted what had happened. Maybe I would have let some emotions out, cried, shouted, screamed, felt some anger, told someone, anyone, how I was feeling, but I didn't know how to tell people, family, teachers or Priest how I felt.

Lollipops, Bubblegum, Death and Lies

So this was how I coped, by shutting off, just as I always had, and continued to do, with what John had done to me, and carried on doing to me.

Mum and Dad came home from the funeral, and Mum looked drained. There was no word to me as to how it had gone, but I noticed that Mum was wearing a small ring on her little finger, it was tight and didn't quite reach the base of the finger. When I asked where she got it from, she told me it was Susan's, and that Elwyne had given it to her. I don't know how true that was, but I had never seen it before, neither had I ever seen Susan wearing it.

That was it, all over. Now all we needed was the healing process, but it wasn't over for me, far from it. I felt so isolated that no one was paying any attention to me or my needs to talk. I still didn't rebel, I wasn't rude to my elders, I even continued to comply with John's wishes. I don't think that there was any such thing as counselling in those days, but, if there was in 1959, I don't think anyone ever sought advice on my behalf.

About six months after Susan had died, I remember going from Kingshurst to Birmingham with Mum on the bus. I was aware that the passengers were talking to their companions, I was aware that Mum was by my side, and I was aware that the conductor had been for his fare. I watched the passing traffic and I started to daydream amidst the hubbub of sound. I was day dreaming that, wickedly, the bus that we were on would have a bad crash, that I would be seriously hurt. There would be firemen, police and ambulance men tending to me, with all the attention being directed only to me, and I would be taken to hospital where doctors and nurses would be looking after me. This day dream happened on many occasions, and lasted for many years.

When I was day dreaming like this I felt a sense of security, a belonging, that my needs were being met, but inside I was screaming, and I couldn't tell anyone. I wouldn't know where to start or how to put my thoughts into the words that I wanted to say, or could it have been, maybe, that I thought that I also needed to be hurt, and that like Susan, who had felt a terrific amount of pain, I needed to feel it also, to know what Susan had gone through.

Life carried on, dare I use the phrase, 'as normal'. I carried on going to school, though I was getting a lot of tummy aches, head aches, tooth aches, leg aches, arm aches, bum aches. Anything ached just as long as it merited a day off school. The one thing that did change in the May of 1960, was Mum's gypsy spirit surfacing again, and we moved flat, diagonally in the same block!.

Mum was still working nights at the G.E.C, Witton. She claimed that the young family living above us were too noisy, and she was finding it hard to sleep during the day, and so put in for a transfer. By chance, the family that lived at 49 Ash Crescent were also looking for a transfer, and so a straight swap took place. I became friends with their daughter Eunice who was about the same age as me. Although she didn't go to the same school as me, we played together in the afternoons after school.

It was during my last three terms at junior school that I changed school yet again, and I was moved to St. Anthony's R.C school that was located at the bottom of the Estate. There was one teacher there who I looked upon as a surrogate mum, named Mrs O'Sullivan. She was big and round, immaculately dressed, wore clip-on ear rings, and spoke softly. There was always a jar of sweets on her desk, a reward for the pupils who tried their best. (I think that many a dentist would frown on this lovely lady for her reward system).

She would often give me little jobs around the classroom, sharpening pencils, filling the inkwell on her desk, watering the plants that were located on the window sills, and she even secured for me the job of washing the staff members cups and saucers after break. I wanted to throw my arms around her ample shape and feel, what I imagined to be her warmth, but I knew this could never happen. I often wonder, if I had slipped my arms around her waist, would I have opened up, would I have told her everything?. Even if I did tell her, would she be able to understand the turmoil, or would she see me as some kind of pathetic little creature who was making up these 'stories' about John and Susan?. I don't suppose I would have risked telling her, and anyway, I only had perhaps two, maximum three terms at this school.

In this year nature told me that I was growing up, and I began to develop 'pubes' in my nether regions. I was so naïve, that I thought I was changing sex!, so I took a pair of scissors to my fuzz and cut it all off, hoping that it would never return, however, The 'Forest of Dean' still remains. If I thought that was bad, there was worse to come, oh yes... Periods. Mum never told me about periods, (if she thought ignorance was bliss, she was wrong), and when I told her I was bleeding her reply was, "Oh you're 'so-so'', (What the bloody hell is 'so-so'?), anyway she produced a pad, or as Mum called it an S.T, and an elastic 'G' string (ha-ha), with two hooks on it, one at the back and one at the front, and told me to put it on,...and for how long, for, a day, a week, a month...forever?. Eventually my own initiative told me. Mum did, however, offer me some words of 'wisdom', which were, 'don't bath, and don't wash your hair when having a period, or else you will go mad in later life!!.

Just as nature was playing around with the bottom half of my body, she started on the top half as well, as my boobs went from the size of pimples to the size of tennis balls, in what seemed to me, overnight. I swear the Good Lord up above had too much flesh left over after making millions of other people, and stood with it in his hands, looking at it as if to say, 'What the bloody hell do I do with the leftovers'. Then he spotted me down below, and thought, 'here you are love, you can have this lot !', and because since then I have never been small in the 'Titty' department, I have hated the size of them all my life.

Stan and Marie had moved out, and they

were living in 'digs' at Stetchford, Birmingham. Dad was at work, and Mum had gone into Birmingham to do some shopping. I was on a period, and so I did not go with her as I was feeling unwell. I heard her going into John's bedroom, and she told him she was off to town and wouldn't be too long, and that I was asleep in bed as I wasn't feeling too good, then I heard the front door close and she was gone. As I turned over, I heard my bedroom door open and I turned to see John standing there,... Christ, he didn't waste any time!. He asked me what was wrong with me, but I was NOT going to tell HIM my personal problems, I was not going to tell him I was bleeding, so I just told him I wasn't very well. He then climbed into bed with me, and although I told him 'No!', he still put his arm round my waist. I turned to face him and told him that I was on a period, as I honestly thought this would make him get out of bed, but he didn't. Instead, as before, he guided my hand down to his penis, cupped my hand round his shaft, and he told me to 'wank' him off, so I complied, thinking that once he'd had enough he would leave me alone. Only this time was different, he was lying on his back, and as I was rubbing his penis up and down my wrist was aching. I obviously wasn't going fast enough for him, because he placed his hand over the top of mine and moved it faster, all the time making noises, not loud, but murmuring indistinguishable sounds. Then it happened, his head came forward and he said he was 'coming', and white stuff went over his and my hands. I thought he'd wet himself, and I felt nauseous, this 'stuff' was sticky, and I didn't know what to do with it. He told me it was alright, it was called 'spunk', and it happens to all men, 'now go and wash it off,…and don't tell Mum and Dad!'.

I went into the bathroom to wash my hands and watched as my sins disappeared down the plughole. My stomach turned somersaults, I felt sick, and as I dried my hands, I rubbed and rubbed as hard as I could, so much that I made my hands go red and sore. As I looked at myself in the mirror, I once again felt so disgusted with myself and so ashamed. For fear of John trying to do anything to me again, even though I was feeling rough, I got dressed and went into the living room. Although I loved him as a brother and sister should, with all the bickering, teasing and hating him in the next sentence, his meaning of loving me was obviously totally different to mine.

As usual, nothing was said, and when Mum came home I told her I was feeling better. She gave me some sweets, and I picked up my roller skates and asked if could go out and play with a couple of friends. Nothing was showing on me, I'd washed the 'spunk' away, and I'd tucked away what had happened into some dark and murky place in my brain. I hadn't got a sign on my forehead that said 'just done a hand job', so it was carry on as usual in my childlike status. I put all my efforts into skating that day, and as I rushed around on them, I could feel the wind in my hair, blowing across my forehead. Maybe it would blow away the memory?.

Chapter 8

MADNESS ALL AROUND

John was never one to hold down a job. But in 1960, I don't know whether it was national conscription, or whether he decided to give the army a try, but I remember him packing his case, and Mum saying good bye to him. No sooner had the front door closed, than Mum turned on me, and told me it was my fault that he was joining the forces. She never explained herself, and I never asked her why. This cold shoulder response left me bewildered, especially when she started to cry, and I didn't know whether to cuddle her and risk being shrugged off, or leave her alone, so I decided to leave her alone. I remember thinking, 'I'm safe, he's gone', but no one would tell me how long he would be gone for. The house did seem empty for awhile, kind of quieter. To this day I never understood my Mum's little outburst, and

I still do not know what she meant by the comment that it was my fault,...how?, why?. I still feel hurt by that comment, as I didn't force John to go, or did I?.

Mum needn't have worried, John wasn't away for long, as he managed to get himself discharged by taking an overdose of tablets. This got him the attention he craved, but this harmful activity was to eventually cost him dearly, and he would one day carry his 'attention seeking' too far, only it would not be via an overdose.

Once back home he started to look for another job. He became a male student nurse at a mental Hospital for people with dementia and other mental conditions. Ironically, here was a man who had taken an overdose of tablets just to get a discharge from the forces, and yet, he was going to help people with mental health problems!. How can that one possibly work?, the answer is ..it didn't.

One thing that I will say in his defence, he put his heart and soul into this job. He would revise when he came home, disappearing into his bedroom, often leaving his tea to be heated up at 10.00 pm, Then he'd eat his tea and settle down for the night. When he woke the next day, he would do an hours revision again before leaving for work at the hospital.

The one thing that he always had difficulty with, was detaching himself from the patients. There was an elderly lady there named Peggy, and John would often come home with sweets or chocolate, or biscuits which Peggy had given to him. When Peggy died, he found it hard to cope with, and his way of coping was to take yet another overdose. I'll never know if it was his way of blotting out the pain of losing someone he deemed to be close to, or if the endless revision had finally got too much for him. Whatever the reason, because he had tried to commit suicide, which was, and still remains, against the law, the police were involved, although I don't recall to what extent. John was finally admitted to All Saints Hospital in Winson Green, Birmingham, where he received Electro Convulsive Therapy treatment and a concoction of drugs.

As an adult, I found out that when John was approximately eight years old, he'd been playing in the old 'rec', which was a local park, when a man had sexually assaulted John, and though I don't know anything more than that, I do wonder if that was the core of his later problems.

I don't think the treatment that John received in hospital was of any help. Dad only went once to see him in Hospital, but

Mum and I would go on a regular basis, and as far as I know, we were the only ones to visit him. Whenever I saw him, he looked grey, unhappy, almost vacant, his eyes were glazed, and he seemed very quiet. On the sunny days, we would sit on a bench in the grounds, and Mum would send me off for a walk, I suppose to give her some time with her son, and on other days, if it was overcast or raining, the three of us would go to the hospital cafe and have a drink and a bite to eat.

One day when Mum and I went to visit him, his left wrist was bandaged up to his elbow. John admitted that at a group meeting, he'd had a disagreement with the psychiatric doctor. John said he had got up and left the room, but that his temper had got the better of him, and he'd put his fist through a window pane. That's what he told us, but I have my suspicions. I do wonder, and of course I will never find out, whether he had tried to slit his wrist, and my reason for that suspicion is that he was right handed, and it was his left wrist that was bandaged. Surely if someone is right handed, wouldn't they hit someone or something with their right hand?.

I hated these visits to the hospital, and I was frightened of the way the inmates looked at me. I was frightened of their actions, the sudden outbursts of shouting, the rocking backwards and forwards, the calling out to me, and them having no control over their bodies. I was always so glad when Mum and I were catching the bus home, and I did not want to go and visit him again in that hospital. Wasn't my pleasure of leaving that hospital selfish?, after all, John had to remain there. Did he belong with these people, or was what he was doing to himself, to use the phrase, 'a cry for help'. Even If it was, back then, it would have been classed as madness, and if he had succeeded in committing suicide, then he would have been seen as a coward. So is killing yourself being strong, an act of cowardice, or simply an act that hurts the ones that love you?

Chapter 9

LOLLIPOPS, BUBBLEGUM, AND FIRST LOVE

Elwyne and Fred were struggling to hold on to their failing marriage, and In October 1960 they had another daughter, Lorraine, but If they thought this little bundle of joy was the answer to their problems, they were mistaken, and instead of binding their marriage to make it stronger, the sheer delicacy of the thread was under more strain, until it eventually broke. Fred started drinking more heavily than usual and would on occasions lash out at Elwyne, and whenever the arguments, the physical attacks, or the mental anguish got too much for Elwyne to bear, she took Pamela and Lorraine to the only other safe place she could think of...Mum and Dad's. As a ten year old child, I thought it exciting to have my big sister and my little nieces stay with us. Pamela shared the small bedroom with me,

Elwyne and Lorraine were in with Mum, and Dad would be in with John, who was by now home from All Saints Hospital.

Fred would come and knock on the front door, but Elwyne would refuse to speak to him. Mum would never invite him in, and Dad would try and reason with Elwyne to speak to him, but Elwyne would not be swayed. Curiosity would always get the better of her though, and she would look out of the living room window to see Fred standing on the pavement below, collar turned up and looking really sorry for himself. She would eventually go down to him, and once Fred had gone, Elwyne returned back to the flat, and she would tell Mum and Dad that they were going to give their marriage one more try. So the next day, Pamela and Lorraine would leave again with Elwyne, but two or three months down the line they would be back with us, and the process would start over again.

In 1961, May or June time, I sat the national eleven plus examinations, the exam that sorted out the 'brains' from the 'thicko's,... guess which category I fell into, no Grammar school for me then!. Along with countless others, I had failed. (I had failed on purpose, don't you know ?!!), so in September 1961, I went to St Pauls R.C. school, in Coleshill,

Warwickshire. I was a 'big' girl, and had to wear a maroon colour BOYS blazer, (because the girls blazers only went up to a 34" chest and I was a 36" chest at eleven years old!), a grey skirt, blue blouse, and white three-quarter length socks. God, what a mess I looked, Overweight, glasses, long hair. Was it any wonder that I didn't take much notice of things, for if I had, I might not have coped as well as I did in my teenage and adult years.

The teachers at this school seemed antiquated to me, and had names to suit their personality, like Mr Moody, (speaks for itself, eh?), or Mrs Warral, P.E. teacher (War like!). Miss Bright taught Domestic Science, bless her, she must have carried the nails for Noah she was that old, but unlike her name, she seemed anything but bright. The one teacher that filled me with dread was our sewing teacher, Mrs Cotterill. I started to make a blouse whilst in her lessons, but by the time I had finished (2 years later!!), I had gone from a 36" to a 38" bust . She would never let me use the electric sewing machines, no, those were reserved for her favourites, so I had to use an old treadle machine, and the bloody thing always went backwards when I used it, rendering my hard work useless, so I had to start the process over again!.

Lollipops, Bubblegum, Death and Lies

God give me strength, I hate sewing even today, and I can do anything with a needle and cotton except sew!. Mr Moody taught art, music and poetry. He would not think twice about using the 'strap', and stood for no nonsense off anyone. Both boys and girls would get the same treatment if he thought it was merited.

At 11 stone in weight, P.E. always posed a problem for me. When it came to using the 'spring board', I always imagined breaking it as I took a running jump ready to vault over the 'horse'. One day, as I kept changing places in the queue with other kids, the teacher noticed that I had not had my turn. She was not in the least bit encouraging, instead she told me to get a move on and jump over the 'horse'. I knew that I would not be able to do it and played for time, but with a stern warning about me going to the headmasters office, which inevitably would result in the strap, I decided there was nothing for it but to try. I ran up to the spring board, grabbed both handles on the horse, and I managed to tuck my legs up,but not quite high enough!. My feet caught the side of the horse, and still holding onto the handles, I started to fall backwards, bringing the horse with me. As I fell, in what seemed to be slow motion, my hands seemed 'glued' to the handles and the horse landed on top of me, winding me, and breaking one of the lenses in my glasses. The broken glass cut me just over the top of my eyebrow, and even with blood seeping down my face, there were no words of apology, just 'go and clean it up'. I hated her for what she had just made me do, but to me the worst thought was, what on earth was I going to tell my Mum?, I don't know about a ruler being shoved up her arse, Mum would have killed that teacher and taken the consequences. I could hide the wound on my forehead with my fringe, but the glasses were not so easy to hide, besides which I could not do without them. I explained this away, by saying that I had dropped them as I was being jostled onto the coach on our way home, an explanation that was accepted by Mum, but today's 'OFSTED' would have had a field day with this school.

The staff there were strict, and we had assembly every morning before lessons, where good guide lines were set down in the form of hell and damnation. We were taught good morals, how to keep our hearts and souls pure, and to do this, a good catholic child who wanted to secure a place next to God, was to go to Confession and pray to

Lollipops, Bubblegum, Death and Lies

Our Lady for forgiveness, and through her we would get to God's holy place. Well, that's me out then, as I never confessed to taking Susan's life, and no way was I going to tell anyone of my deepest sin with John. At the age of eleven, I really didn't know which secret was worse....Susan or John.

In late 1962, although still very much into lollypops, bubblegum, roller skates and skipping ropes, I began to notice boys, especially the ones who were a couple of years above me at school. There was one very special one, who, although he didn't go to my school, lived opposite us, and he saw past my size and glasses. I would play hide and seek with him and his sisters, and he and I would go and hide, then one day, he kissed me, not the tonsil tickling sort, but the sweet innocent sort, mouths closed, no touching intimate parts sort of kiss. I experienced a sense of guilt and elation at the same time, as how could anyone like me enough to kiss me the sweet way he had just done?. How long did this first love last?, let me think back,...oh yes, two weeks maximum, but long enough for me , for once in my life, to feel special.

Back at school, I would do the good catholic thing and go to confession, but always omitting the 'incest' that was a part of my life, and omitting the part I played in Susans death. Every Thursday the whole school would walk up Coleshill High Street and past various 'children's care homes', and onto St. Paul's church. If we had been to confession the weekend before, then we could receive the 'Holy Host', however, If we hadn't been to confession, not only could you not receive the communion, but you could feel holes were being 'bored' into the back of your head by the teachers. Once back in the classroom, anyone who had not received the communion that morning was asked why and then given a lecture, which often turned into 'blah-blah-blah', as I learned to 'switch off'.

I began to feel insecure, and I didn't want to go to school, but to stay at home with Mum. Before going to school I would kiss Mum, and I would just touch her hand in an attempt to take an essence of her with me, before leaving to catch the coach for school. Once out of the house I would not touch anything with my hands for fear of rubbing off what I could only imagine then as the 'germs' that had been transferred from Mum's hand to mine. Even when I went to the loo, I would not wash my hands afterwards, and the only things I ever touched were my own exercise books, and my own pencils and pencil case.

No one else was allowed to use my pencils, and I didn't want to use theirs either, as I didn't want anyone else to share my Mum's 'germs'. I would ask others to open doors for me, using the excuse that I had hurt my hand, and I would walk up the stairs not placing my hands on the banister. Only when I arrived home from school, did I feel it was safe for me to wash my hands, but the next day the whole process would start again. If I did need to touch anyone else's hand, for example, when we did country dancing, then I would sulk, or go into a mood, and feel as though I had been robbed of my 'germy' security.

Chapter 10

PLAYGROUND TALK

Although I had other friends at school, I was closer to one girl more than the rest, her name was Jean, and she was the youngest of three children. She had a brother who was six years older than her, and a sister who was four years older. I felt an admiration for Jean, as her sister used to talk to her about her boyfriends, and because of this, Jean was more sexually enlightened than me, whereas I ,on the other hand, was still very naive. One day, in the 'girls only' playground, we were talking about sex, and I blurted out a question, I wanted to know, 'does a black man have black spunk?'. Strangely, as soon as the last word had left my mouth, I felt inexplicably sick, and did I really want to know?. Jean thought this was very funny, called me a daft sod, and told me, 'no, his spunk is white, the same as a white mans!'.

Lollipops, Bubblegum, Death and Lies

I could have cried for asking such a stupid question, I was nearly thirteen, not three, and I should have known the answer to that question, but I didn't. How could anyone, who was already accustomed to sexual acts, not have known the answer?. The school bell rang and we lined up ready to go to our next lesson, but all the way through the lesson I kept wondering why I had wanted to know the answer to the question. Why when I thought of John and his 'deposits' on my hand, would I even want to ask a question like that?. I felt really stupid, and the familiar feeling of being dirty came washing over me again. One thing is for certain, if we'd had sex education back then, I might not have felt the need for school playground 'tittle-tattle'.

In 1963 I became a teenager, and Mum and Dad bought me my first pair of 'grown up' shoes which were tan coloured, and boasted a small 1"heel, I loved them and because of the heel, I felt really 'grown up'. I was also allowed to go to a youth club which was held at the Guardian Angels, the school I had attended some four years earlier. I went with a couple of friends off the estate, leaving home at 7.00pm, and having to be back home by 9.00pm, not a minute later, or I wouldn't be allowed to go next week, simple as that.

It cost me 6d to get in (2.1/2p), and with 1/- left (5p), I had enough left for two orange squash drinks. People would dance to Chubby Checker, who would encourage us to 'Twist again', and Tony Mehan and Jet Harris, Elvis Presley, Bobby Darrin, and many more artists who's names have become obscured through time. I enjoyed going for the company, but I could never get up and dance, no, that was left to the more confident, better looking, better dressed girls. I had Just about one hour there, then it was time to go home, to ensure being back before 9.00pm.

One Friday evening, I came home from the club to see a police car outside our block of flats, but little did I know that the police were at my house. Yes, John had taken yet another overdose, and he was lying on his back with the police trying to get him onto his side. Mum and Dad were calling his name, slapping his hands, and trying to wake him up. I was shocked and frightened by what I was witnessing, and I called out his name, but I was ushered out by the police who asked me to watch out for the ambulance. When it arrived I ran back to the bedroom and told them, and one of the policemen went out to direct the ambulance men to the bedroom. From there, with the combined efforts of the police and the ambulance men, they got John to the ambulance, and as far as I know, once at the hospital he had his stomach pumped, and was then hospitalised once again at All Saints.

Mum and Dad never did tell me who found him, or why John did these things, and I didn't ask. I just went to bed and assumed that our visits to see John in hospital would soon start over again, and I thought to myself, 'how could he put Mum and Dad through all of this?'. Didn't he know how much Mum was hurting, Did he care even?. But then, the only care that was available for people with mental issues back then was to lock them away from society, after all there was no counselling, that is unless you could afford to go to a private doctor, and that only seemed to apply to M.P's and Managing directors, and the like.

Sure enough, our visits soon started, and again, I always felt uneasy about going. Ironically John was always drugged up, even though the very reason for him being in this hospital was because of his drug overdose, but I supposed that the only difference between him taking an overdose at home, and him being dosed-up in hospital, was that he was able to be monitored. The other treatment apparently given to him again was E.C.T. (Electro Convulsive Therapy), in which John was strapped to a bed, where he was given an injection to make him drowsy, had electrodes fitted to his head, then electrical currents were passed through the wires to stimulate the brain activity or patterns. It was supposed to make a difference or to alter the mood of the patient, but I don't know how it worked, or even if it did work,...I doubt it.

I began to feel the pressure of these hospital visits, and I vowed back then that a 'mental breakdown' would never happen to me, I would NOT allow it. I was NEVER going to go anywhere near a place like that, where people looked like something that had been dug up, where they had no control over their life, and were virtually imprisoned. This second time round, visiting times frightened me just as much as they had the first. I couldn't really comprehend what was going on, but I do know that my fear and hatred for these mental institutions still holds a dread.

On his return from hospital again, we 'pussy footed' around John, wondering when he would do the next stupid thing, and again, when no one was around, he would take me to bed. I still don't know why, perhaps I felt sorry for him, and felt that if I complied with his lustful wishes then he wouldn't put Mum and Dad through the agony, torment and pain of him overdosing again. I lay on my back waiting and he told me to open my legs. Shivering, I did so, and he asked me if I was cold, but I just shook my head, I wasn't cold, I was scared stiff, and I didn't want to do these things. He placed his fingers inside me again and asked if it was nice, but I closed my eyes, not wanting to look at him, and I switched off and felt nothing. Then he got on top of me and placed his penis just inside my vulva, he was groaning, I wished it was all over, and I told myself that it soon would be. I could feel him thrusting his penis up and down, and I could feel his breath in my ear, but I didn't dare open my eyes. Then as he groaned he let out a sigh, and it was then that I felt something trickle down to my bottom. I pushed him off with every bit of strength I'd got, and he just lay there while I shouted at him, asking him what he'd done. He told me that he'd 'come' between my legs, so I ran to the bathroom and washed everything away, still shaking, I was worried, and I felt sick.

After the talks I'd had with Jean in the playground, I now knew that to become pregnant, a man had to 'make love' to you, and that his sperm had to go into the vagina.

Even though I was now thirteen, I still didn't fully grasp the 'concepts' of conception, but as my mind raced, I worried that because the sperm had trickled past my vagina, and round to my bottom, some of the sperm could have trickled up there, and that there was a possibility that I was pregnant.

As I came out of the bathroom, and headed toward the stairs to go down, John called me to go back to him, but I said 'no'. He told me that he wasn't going to do anything, he just needed to talk to me, so I went to the bedroom and stood by the door. Finding that he was dressed and sitting on the edge of the bed, his head bowed down, with him looking at the floor, I snapped, 'what!?'. I certainly wasn't prepared for what he was going to ask me to do, and I remember him looking at me as I stood and waited, studying me, his face questioning and serious, and he said, 'Pray to God to kill me'. I couldn't really understand what he was trying to say, and I cried there and then, 'I want you to promise me', he said, but I told him to shut up. No matter what John had done to me, I didn't want my brother dead, and I remembered all those years ago, when John asked me to show his friend my 'fanny', how could it have gone from that request to the one he was asking of me now?. I just didn't understand, but I guess he must have had an inkling that what he was doing just might be wrong. When I looked into his eyes, there were no tears, his ginger hair was ruffled, and I now wonder if it was all just for the attention, just as the overdosing had been. As I left him there in the room I felt wicked, as although I didn't want him dead, I knew that I would be free if he did die, but it would not be me that did the praying...not yet anyway.

Chapter 11

ANOTHER MOVE, SAME OLD SEX

I don't know whether Mum and Dad felt that they had to get away from this area because of the embarrassment, shame, and stigma of having a 'loopy' son, but there was a phase of new buildings taking place at the far end of Kingshurst, so Mum and Dad applied for one of the new maisonettes that were being built. They went to view one at 82 Oakthorpe Drive, which Dad thought it was brilliant. Mum had her reservations, and she didn't like it, but with Dad's persuasion they went ahead with the move, and although it was yet another home for me, I remained at the same school. In the weeks prior to the move, we would cart small items, by hand, down the road to the maisonette, things like ornaments, crockery, spare curtains, towels, and store them in the various cupboards around the house, so that when the time for the actual move came, there would be less for us to do. The maisonette had three bedrooms, a bathroom, separate toilet, a kitchen large enough to house a dining table, and a living room with 'French' windows that led into our own garden. John had the front bedroom, I had the small room, and Mum and Dad had the largest room.

Elwyne and Fred were still trying to make an effort with their marriage, and by this time were renting a council house in Kingshurst Way, not a great distance from us. I still wasn't liked by Fred, and so Elwyne would usually visit Mum when Elwyne was on her own, or with Pamela and Lorraine, and I suppose that it kept Fred and me at a distance. Their time on Kinghurst was only short lived, as not long after our move to Oakthorpe Drive, they moved to Pittfield Road, in Kitts Green. I do wonder if us moving into close proximity to them had anything to do with them moving away!

Mum had changed her job again, only this time she was working days. Dad used to go out of the house at 6.30am as he worked in Harbourne, in Birmingham. Mum was out of the house by 7.00am, and I didn't go out until 8.15am to catch the coach for school. One morning I got up and made breakfast for myself, had my wash, then came down the stairs and stood by the large chiffonier that was standing in the hallway, where I started to comb my hair. In the mirror, I noticed John coming down the stairs, and I don't know why he wasn't at work, but he stood at the foot of the stairs looking at me. He told me to come up stairs, and again, don't ask me why, I just complied, even though I knew what he was going to do, there were no excuses for my part. He went into Mum and Dad's bedroom where the bed had been made, undid the blankets, then undressed, and I automatically felt mentally switched off. He climbed naked into Mum and Dad's bed, and told me to get in beside him, even though I was fully clothed. As I lay on my back, he pulled my top up and slid my bra over the top of my boobs, he rubbed them, then he told me to take off my knickers. I wanted 'it' over with, and the quicker I did 'it', the sooner I would get away. He put his fingers inside my vulva and started manipulating them, then the usual question followed, 'was it nice?', God I felt sick, of course it wasn't nice, it was wrong. He then rolled on top of me, squashing my tits against his chest, slid his penis inside me and thrust himself up and down. He must have thought it OK to do the same as he had the last time, and again the sperm slid down to my bottom. When he had finished, he lay on his back, but I was now used to his sick ways, as again he asked me to pray to God to take his life.

I went into the bathroom and cleaned myself up, as I didn't want any part of him on me, then I broke down and cried silently. As I looked at myself in the bathroom mirror, I hated what I saw, I was thirteen years old, going into fourteen, so why couldn't I fight him?. I needed to compose myself, so I took my time, and by the time I left the bathroom, John had made Mum and Dad's bed, leaving no trace of the sin that had just taken place.

By now it was too late for me to go to school, the coach would have left taking my friends with it, I hated school, but, today, God I wished I was on that coach taking me there!. My reward for being a 'good' girl was the day off school and neither of us would say anything to Mum and Dad. For the rest of the day I was in a sullen mood, and John acted as though nothing had happened, but going through my mind for the first time was the thought that I now hated him, and I hated with a vengeance what he was doing, but then again, today I had still gone willingly.

That was the first time in my life I had such bad feelings about him, and felt in my mind that perhaps I should pray for his death. Wicked or what?. I also vowed that this time was the last. No more!, I would avoid, or at least try to avoid him as much as I could, even though I knew that would be difficult living in the same household, but believe me, I would do it.

That day, I stayed in my bedroom listening to my records, looking at the posters of pop stars that I had pinned to my bedroom wall, and I became angry at my own weakness. I didn't eat that lunchtime because I didn't want to see John, he might just come into the kitchen at the same time that I was preparing something to eat, and I didn't want to chance it.

When Mum came home, I made sure my school satchel was left on the chair along with my coat, to make it look as if I had been to school. She told me to hang my coat on the hook and take my satchel up stairs into my bedroom, or hang it up with my coat, and not to clutter up the living room. Mum prepared the tea, and after eating, as I could not bear to be in the same room as John now, I washed up for Mum and then I told her that I was going to listen to my records.

With the music playing softly, I cried again. My emotions were in absolute turmoil, and though in my mind I called John all the names under the sun, I still felt that I must take some of the blame for what was happening to me. At nine pm, I shouted down stairs that I was settling down to sleep, as I did not want my Mum or Dad to see the redness of my eyes. If they started asking me questions, how could I have answered them?, no doubt with yet another lie!.

The next day, my form teacher asked why I wasn't at school the day before, so I lied through my teeth, and told him that I had over slept and missed the coach. He said that he would want a letter from my Mum to that effect, but I told him that I had lost it, and would get another one,......I never did.

Chapter 12

ONE MENTAL HOSPITAL IS THE SAME AS ANOTHER

Stan and Marie were having a house built in Stourbridge, Worcestershire, and in 1964 they left their 'digs' and came back to live with us in Oakthorpe Drive until the completion of their house in May/June of that year. Of course we had to rearrange the bedrooms, so with single beds put into Mum and Dads bedroom, John moved into there with Dad, Stan and Marie then had John's room, and Mum and I were squeezed into the little bedroom.

One Saturday, I went out with my friends around the estate, and when I came home there was an ambulance outside our house. I immediately thought that John was up to his tricks again, but this time the ambulance wasn't for him, it was for Mum. Mum was not in the best of health, and never did look after herself properly. She was overweight, ate all the wrong foods and smoked, her health was deteriorating, and she had varicose veins, which eventually developed into an ulcerated leg. On this particular Saturday, Dad had come home from work, and as Mum walked in from doing the shopping, she told Dad that her legs felt swollen and sore. Dad went into the kitchen to make her a cup of tea, and apparently, as Mum went to lift her legs up onto another chair to rest them, the ulcer had ruptured. I walked into the house fully expecting to see John collapsed, but the sight that greeted me was one of blood on the floor, and there were even splatters on the ceiling. The ambulance men were dealing with Mum, while Stan and John were helping as best as they could, trying to clear up the mess.

Mum was taken into Birmingham General Hospital. She had lost four pints of blood, and was in a bad condition. It was touch and go as to whether she would make it or not, and she stayed in hospital for three weeks. Between us all, we coped with the mundane housework, such as washing, ironing, meals etc., but thank God that Stan and Marie were living with us at that time, otherwise, with just Dad, me ,and John at home, when Dad went out to work John would have had 'free range' of me. I feel they were my saviours without them ever knowing it.

When Mum came home again, there was no holding her down. As usual, she took it easy for a few weeks, then found herself another job, this time as a general cook at the Alexandra Theatre, in Birmingham, where she would start her work at 4.00 pm and finish at 10.00pm.

Some Saturdays, I was lucky enough to go with her to the theatre where I met some famous people of the times, The Batchelors, an Irish singing trio, John Alderton, Morcambe and Wise, some of the Royal Ballet company, and Sadlers and Wells Opera company. I even earned myself some cash, when one of the 'dressers' for the cast of the Opera company was away ill and I was asked to go to the wardrobe department and help with the dressing of the 'stars'. I really enjoyed myself in the time I was doing that job. The Back Stage Manager asked if I would like to see backstage,...'I certainly would !', so I went backstage and I got the chance to do a bit of 'striking and setting' on the stage when a scene needed changing. I loved it immensely, and I earned 10/- for the privilege!.

Frank Avenell, an ATV manager asked when I was due to leave school, and I told

Lollipops, Bubblegum, Death and Lies

him not until July,1965. He then told me that if I wanted a job in Make-up, I should contact him, and he would get me into the Max factor school for make-up artists. I believed him and hadn't any reason to doubt him, but because of the events that would take place in the near future, it was never going to happen

John found himself a job with the M.E.B. as a meter reader, and part of his job was to collect money from the meters, and access houses to take the readings for the people who paid their bills at the office. He started to make a life for himself, going to clubs and meeting people at last, and he even found himself a girlfriend, although the relationship didn't last long for what ever reason, and I think, that for him, it was the straw that broke the camels back.

Not long after that, one Sunday, we were all up, but John had been out the night before, so he was having a lay in. Mum took a cup of coffee up to him, and then all hell broke loose when she shouted 'Sid!', and my Dad ran upstairs. Stan and Marie came to see what the commotion was about, and I just ambled upstairs, as Stan then ran downstairs and out into the street to the nearest phone box. When I reached Dad and John's bedroom, I could see John, slumped half in and half out of the bed, and tablets scattered on the floor. Not again?, ...It was all very boring by now.

The police and ambulance were called, but this time I didn't cry, I didn't call his name, I just stood and thought, with a shrug of the shoulders, 'well, it's what he wants'. By this time, I was beginning to realise that he had not only hurt me, both physically and mentally, but he was hurting my Mum and Dad too, and although I didn't like what I was witnessing, I just felt 'if your going to do it, just hurry up and do it...put us all out of our misery'. Even then though, in an odd sort of way, because he was my big brother I still loved him, but not in the way he wanted me to.

After the ambulance had left with John, I went into my bedroom and put my records on. I was feeling melancholy, and I questioned myself as to why he felt that he had to hurt the people that loved him. Mum loved her son so much, she would, I'm sure, have forgiven him anything. John was sent to hospital again, only this time he was sent to Hatton Hospital, near to Warwick. I don't know why it wasn't All Saints again, because that would certainly have been closer for mine and Mum's visits, as Hatton Hospital was a three bus ride marathon journey away, and If a connection was missed, it seemed like hours before the next bus was

Lollipops, Bubblegum, Death and Lies

due. So our visits to see John usually became an all-day event, but were they appreciated?...I don't think so!.

This hospital was no different to All Saints, with its grey walls, grey inmates, sombre atmosphere, the shouting, the rocking back and forth, the people staring, and the staff occasionally rushing about. I had got to the stage where I couldn't be bothered to talk to John, and as I had nothing to say to him, I left the conversation to Mum. He just could not, or would not see what he was doing to her. As usual, Dad would never visit John in Hospital, and I don't ever recall him asking Mum when she got home, how his son was. The pressure on Mum to visit John, look after the rest of the family, and go out to work, must have been enormous. After all, no one else went to visit John, and I suppose that any mother would walk to hell and back, if it meant she got to see one of her 'chicks', even if only for a few short hours.

When John came out of Hospital, things between him and Dad were very strained. Dad no longer trusted John to be out late, and so, even though John was twenty one years old, Dad laid the law down. He told him that whilst he lived under his roof, then John would be home by eleven o'clock at the latest, no 'ifs or buts', the law had been laid down. John became very friendly with our cousin, Margaret, to the point that a relationship was formed, of which I think Dad felt shamed, there was an big argument, and Dad told John to his face that he was 'no son of his'. I have always hated arguments, so I put my coat on and went out to my friend's house, where we did what most fourteen-going on eighteen year olds do, we talked about pop stars, listened to records, and had a crafty puff on her Mum and Dads cigarettes which she had 'pinched', one for me and one for her. She threw open the window and blocked the door with a chair, telling her Mum that she was searching for something. She told me about her five brothers, about how unfair it was that only she had to help out with all the chores, but even then she still loved each of them. I do remember telling her that I didn't love my brother, and that he just got on my nerves, though I never did tell her the real reason why I didn't love him.

When I got back home, I fully expected John to be either sprawled out in an overdose induced coma, or having left home, but neither had happened, he was still at home and still breathing. Having John at home, was like walking on egg shells, the whole thing was, as always, a delicate situation.

Chapter 13

YET AGAIN I'M HURTING

Stan and Marie were still living with us, though Stan was no longer in the merchant navy, but was working for a large company called Fisher-Ludlow. Marie used to spend a lot of time in their bedroom, but would occasionally go into Birmingham with Mum on a Saturday. Her command of the English language would make us laugh, as she would say thing like, 'uppy up' for 'wipe up', she would call Mum 'mamma', and Dad she called 'pappa'. She would often swear in Portuguese, with Fuddas, Merda, pashasha, and lots more, she smoked, drank brandy and loved salt fish and cabbage soup. She also had a heart of gold and would do anything for you, I liked her a lot and Stan was happy. Once the house in Stourbridge was ready for them to move into, and their baby was born, then their happiness would be complete.

I was still managing to avoid John, and if he came home before Mum and Dad, I would beat a hasty retreat to a friends house. If her family were about to sit down for their evening meal, they would tell me to go home whilst they ate their tea. If this did happen, I wouldn't go home, but hung around outside, or walked the streets for awhile until I thought they might have finished. I would do anything to avoid giving John the opportunity of thinking he could get away with a quick grope or shag, and from now on, as far as I was concerned, my 'half-penny' was my own!!.

March 21st 1965, the first day of spring, and after working all week, including a Saturday, it wasn't unusual for Dad to have a lay in bed on the Sunday. This particular Sunday, when I came down stairs, Mum asked me not to play my music too loud, or make too much noise, because, she informed me, Dad wasn't feeling too well. I went into his bedroom to ask if he wanted anything to eat or drink, and he told me that I was to ask Mum if she would make some egg custard for him, nothing more. I went down stairs and told Mum of his request, and whilst she busied herself making his egg custard, I went back upstairs and quietly listened to my radio. When Mum took it up to him, she called for John and told him to go to the phone box and call for the doctor, as Dad was having chest pains. John soon came back and told Mum that the doctor was on his way. I wondered what was going on, but all Mum said was that I was not to worry, and that Dad would be OK.

When Doctor Cranston arrived he talked to Dad, then gave him a shot of morphine. He wanted Dad to go to Hospital, but Dad told him that he didn't want to go. When the Doctor came down stairs I heard him tell Mum that Dad had suffered a heart attack, and ideally he should go into hospital. Doctor Cranston said that he did not want to put any pressure on Dad, for fear of making things worse, then he left, telling Mum not to hesitate in calling him if things did not improve. Just two hours later he was called back again, and he gave Dad another shot of morphine. This time he managed to persuade him that he would be better off in hospital, where there would be specialised equipment that could help him, and I think that my Dad was in so much pain that he just agreed.

Mum, John and I started making a clearing in the bedroom so that a stretcher would have room to pass, as Dr Cranston had told us that a stretcher would be the only way to get Dad down stairs, so that as little strain as possible would be put on Dads heart. We put John's bed on its end, up against the wall, and the chest of drawers was put in front of it, so that the bed was secured, and that left a nice clear walkway for the ambulance men to get the stretcher through. Dad had remained lying flat, and Stan had done a lot of the more strenuous work. Marie was worried, and because by this time she was six months pregnant, she just kept out of the way. I also don't think she could cope with seeing just how much pain Dad was in.

When the ambulance men arrived, instead of the expected stretcher, they brought in a collapsible chair. They got Dad out of bed and wrapped a blanket round him, and once Dad was seated in the chair, they tipped it slightly backwards so that it was resting on two small rear wheels, then they pushed the chair with Dad in it onto the landing. Dad was ashen, he looked awful, and by now his breathing was laboured. One of the ambulance men held onto the back of the chair, and the other went round to the front, taking hold of the base of the chair and tilting it backwards ready to carry it down. They had just managed to get the chair with Dad in it to the bottom of the stairs, when the chair suddenly collapsed beneath him. I shouted 'Dad!', and I was almost in tears, as I rushed down the stairs, but Dad raised a hand to me and told me that he was alright. Whilst Dad was being made a fuss of, and pathetically being reassured that he was going to be alright, and of how sorry the ambulance men were, they eventually got Dad into the ambulance. I thought Mum would go with him, but she didn't, and surprisingly, it was John, the one who was having trouble coping with his own life, let alone coping with someone else's, who went in the ambulance with him. From then on the only thing Mum and I could do was sit and wait for any news about Dad, and listen to hushed voices coming from Stan and Marie's room, Stan no doubt filling Marie in as to the details of what was happening.

I asked Mum if she thought Dad would be OK, and she said that Dr Cranston had told her that if Dad can make it for six weeks, which was the amount of time he would have to spend in hospital, then he would be OK, so Mum and I waited and waited. Eventually John returned home, his eyes red and puffy, and he just looked at Mum and shook his head. Although I didn't understand this particular gesture of someone shaking their head, the look on Mum's face said it all, and I knew then, that my Dad had died. Dad was just 59 years old!. Inwardly I blamed the ambulance men for Dad's early death, as if they had done their job properly, Dad might have made it. Instead he was in Little Bromwich hospital, (now called Heartlands hospital) lying all alone, his life taken from him through the incompetence of those two ambulance men. That feeling however, could never be proved, and perhaps it's only my misguided thoughts make me think in that way. I learned later that Dad never even made it to the hospital, and he had died in the ambulance. So much for the specialist equipment, eh?.

As usual, I didn't want anyone to see me crying, so I went into my bedroom put my record player on, and listened to my records. God how I broke my heart, crying silently, so much so that I found it hard to breathe, my ears popped when I tried to swallow, and the snot ran down towards my mouth. I wanted my Dad back, I wanted Susan back, I picked up my pillow and cried into that, I wanted to scream and scream, and I swore at God. You could stick any loyalty I might ever have had to my religion up your arse now!. There was no God, as, if there was, why couldn't he send my Dad back?, why did he take Susan?. Why did he make John act the way he did?, and why did John want to fuck me, when

Lollipops, Bubblegum, Death and Lies

surely he knew it was wrong?. I knew it was wrong, and I was younger than him, so why couldn't he see it, and why was I hurting so much?.

Mum went into school to let them know that my Dad had died, and she informed them of when the funeral was to be, and that I would be taking that day off. When she went home, I stayed at school and during morning assembly, Mr Martin, the head teacher, mentioned in front of the whole school that Dad had died, and that we must remember him in our prayers. But I didn't want to just 'remember' him, I wanted him back, and though I could feel the tears welling up in my eyes I fought them back. I was going on to fifteen years old, and there was no way I would let my classmates see me cry, and to be seen as a 'cry-baby'. I could not concentrate on any of my lessons all that day, or for the next few days, and In truth I didn't want to be there at all, I just wanted to be at home with my Mum.

Chapter 14

MY FIRST EXPERIENCE OF CREMATION

Inside the house, we were getting ready for the hearse that was carrying Dad's body to arrive. Dad had always been quite blasé about death, and he would often joke about us burying him in the back garden to save on the funeral expenses!. His express wishes were that no one should wear black at his funeral, and that he should be cremated, so instead of the customary black clothes, we wore our normal clothes with a black arm band as a mark of respect. The mood in the house was sombre, people were coming and going, and flowers were being delivered from people who wanted to show their last respects but were unable make it to Dad's funeral, and my sister, Jean who had also emigrated to Canada in 1962, came back home to attend Dad's funeral. All of those flowers in their cellophane wrappers were laid out on the lawn, and It was the only time our garden ever had any flowers in it!

Someone called out that the hearse had arrived, and as I went outside, I stopped in the doorway looking straight ahead, and there in that long black car was the coffin carrying my Dad's body. The boot of the hearse was raised, and the flowers were being picked up by the pall bearers and placed around and on top of the coffin. Neighbours stood talking in low whispers, some had their arms folded, and local children, not in the least affected by what was going on, rode their bikes round and round, watching, but not giving a hoot about the proceedings. One woman made the sign of the cross upon herself, no doubt to offer up a prayer for Dad, and I watched as the car boot was closed again, then someone placed their arm round me, though I don't recall who, and I was led to the waiting car. If this had been any other occasion, I would have relished the height of luxury that this car offered, but it wasn't any other occasion, it was my Dad's last journey.

Mum, Elwyne, Jean, John and I climbed into the limousine that would follow behind the one my Dad was in, and from outside of our house to the end of the street, the chief mourner, dressed in a black suit and a black top hat, walked in front of the cortege. At the end of Oakthorpe Drive, the cars stopped and the chief mourner got back into the hearse, then the cars started up again, and picking up speed we were on our way to Perry Barr Crematorium, Dad's final resting place. On our way there, I wondered why a policeman had saluted us as we went past, another man had made the sign of the cross upon himself, and some older people had simply bowed their heads, later I was to learn that they were all signs of respect.

As the cortege turned right into the crematorium I could see people that I recognised, my Dad's brothers and sisters, my aunts and uncles, people from the MEB, Harbourne, where Dad had worked, and the minister, who was going to perform the service. The car door was opened for us and we got out, then stood around, waiting for the main hearse to open its back door again. Dad's coffin was slid out, being carefully handled by the pall bearers who lifted the coffin onto their shoulders, whilst the minister, in his white garb, bible in hand, waited to receive Dad's lifeless body. When he turned and went into the crematorium, the pall bearers carrying Dad's coffin followed him in, they were in turn

Lollipops, Bubblegum, Death and Lies

followed by Mum, John, Me, Jean, Elwyne and Stan, then Dad's brothers and sisters and a few work colleagues and friends. As the minister began his duty by reciting; 'Yeah though I walk through the valley of the shadow of death I will fear no evil', we all filed into the church behind Dad's coffin. John was one side of me and Mum was the other, and they linked their arms through mine as my tears flowed silently and we took our place at the front of the church. Dads coffin had been placed on to the conveyor belt ready for the cremation, and prayers were said and hymns were sung. After the minister had said a few words of condolence, there was a gentle thud and a whirring sound, then I watched through blurred eyes as Dad's coffin moved forward, and the deep red curtains parted to let my him through. I buried my head into John's chest and sobbed uncontrollably. So that was it, my first experience of a funeral. I had to accept that my Dad had finally gone, but If he was watching from above, (or below!), he would have been laughing at all of us, because he was an atheist, and had always maintained that when he died, We should bury him in an orange box in the back garden, instead of lining other people's pockets. Too bad Dad,

I'm afraid we lined other people's pockets alright on that day!.

Once we were back outside the crematorium, people were coming up to Mum saying, 'What a lovely service', and, 'Don't forget to keep in touch', 'He was a good man', etc. etc. etc., but, back in the limousine, Mum cursed Dad's brothers and sisters, saying that they hadn't wanted to know her when 'Sid' was alive, and that she had no intention of keeping in touch with them now!. So that's how I finally lost all contact with my aunts and uncles and cousins. A few of the people who had attended the funeral came back to our house, and Mum made a pot of tea and got out the cakes and biscuits, but I wanted to get out of the oppressive atmosphere, so I made my excuses and went upstairs to my bedroom, from where I could hear the muffled talking downstairs. People didn't hang around for long, and soon the house was left to just me, Jean, Mum and John once again.

I had the rest of that week off school, and as Jean had the loan of her old boyfriend's car she decided to take her and me shopping. It was like a death race though, because she forgot which way to go round the traffic islands, and also that she had to drive on the left hand side of the road, luckily, back then

Lollipops, Bubblegum, Death and Lies

there wasn't the amount of traffic that is on the road today. Once we were in Birmingham, I felt so grown up being with my big sister, as she had long flowing hair, a trim figure, and always looked immaculately dressed. I on the other hand was still 12st. 12lbs, and a slob, and nothing looked, or even fitted right on me, and as we walked along the street, she'd playfully pat my tummy and tell me to hold it in!. I did so, and bloody hell, it hurt, but even so, Jean kept patting my tummy and encouraging me to 'hold it in', so that by the time she left for Canada two weeks later, I was beginning to 'hold it in' automatically!. On the day Jean returned to Canada, there was no chance of us going to see her off, as she was flying from Heathrow or Gatwick airport, and so it was Jeff, her old boyfriend, who took her to London to make sure she got on the plane safely. When he reported back to Mum that Jean had boarded the plane OK, I really felt that I was alone once again.

Four weeks after Dads death, I had my fifteenth birthday. It was no big deal, and I had no party, but I received birthday cards and money to go and buy what I wanted, although I have no doubt, that being the 'piggy' that I was, I spent it on sweets, and the 'Players Number 6' tipped cigarettes that

I had become accustomed to smoking. Both Mum and John knew that I smoked, they even encouraged it, and John would often give me some 'fags', even without me having to do him any 'favours'. Shortly after Dad had died, Stan and Marie's house was completed, so they moved out to Stourbridge, and this new change meant that John now had his own bedroom back again, I had the small bedroom to myself, and Mum had what was John and Dads room.

During the June of this year, John was at work reading the electricity meters on Kingshurst Estate, when he dropped in for a cup of tea with Maurice, one of his work colleagues. Mum really fussed round them, and I don't know how the relationship took off, but almost over night Maurice was staying at our house, three nights during the week and at the weekends. Mum was only fifty three years old, and I suppose she craved the company, but did Maurice really have to share the same bed as her?. The first time I realised that Maurice was sleeping with her, was when I was going to the loo, as he came out of Mum's bedroom. He was wearing pyjama's, but I was shocked, so I just said 'hello', and retreated back into my bedroom, but not before catching a glimpse of Mum still in bed. What could I say?, I didn't question anything, as I knew that I would have been knocked from here to Kingdom come if I had questioned my Mother, therefore I had to accept the situation, which was that HE was going to be part of the fixtures and fittings in our house from now on!.

Chapter 15

WAGE EARNER

It was in July 1965 that I left school at last, a young adult and ready to face the world. John was trying to lay down the law by telling me what time I had to be in by, and telling me to 'pull my weight' around the house by doing my fair share of the housework. I felt rebellion coming on, I wanted to argue my point and not to listen to anyone else's. Once, when I was going out, I put my skirt on and turned over the waist band so that it shortened the skirt by a couple of inches, and when John noticed this he told me that I was not going out looking like a whore, and told me to let the skirt down again. I shouted at him and told him I would go out the way I wanted to go out, but he stood in front of the door and told me again that I wasn't going out like that. I could feel the anger rising in me, but I told him he'd got his own way, and

I yanked my skirt down, so he stepped aside and I went through the door to freedom. Once round the corner and out of sight, up went the waist band again!,...though I had to make sure that I lengthened it again before I got home, so I think that's one up to me !.

In June, 1965, Marie had given birth to a baby girl, who they named Lourdes Marianne, she was a beautiful, dark haired little thing, and seemed so tiny to me. Stan was over the moon at having a daughter, and she seemed to make his life complete, though I just felt sorry that my Dad was not here to see his fourth granddaughter, he really would have loved her.

In August, Mum was looking for a job for herself, and she told me that I was to go with her, as it was time that I thought about finding myself a job. We went to the B.S.A. at Mackadown Lane, Kitts Green, and although there wasn't a job for Mum, there was a job for a clerk/typist which I was interested in, so I was told to go back on the following Monday and the job was mine. It was the only time I have ever been in the right place at the right time. I felt that there was a world of adulthood waiting just for me, and I imagined all the things that I could do with my first weeks wage, these wages were going to buy me the world!. I could have whatever I wanted,.....well as far as £4.17.6d would get me at least!!.

I worked in an office within the factory itself, and my boss was a quiet man, Mr Lloyd, for whom I was to type up letters and also to go round the factory collecting the tallies from the machine workers for completed work. I was basically still quite shy, and it was deemed funny by the male machinists to bang down the guards of their machines, and make me jump with fright when I was nearby. However I loved the job and the work, even though the other 'girls' in the office seemed really old to me. There was Vera, Joan, and Carmel, whom I am pleased to say accepted me into the fold and gave me useful advice. I would leave the house at 6.45am, 'clock' in at 7.30am, and finished at 5.00 pm, so I would be back in the house by 5.45pm. Once I'd eaten my tea, I would go out with my friends, but Mum would want me back in the house by 9.00 pm on a week day, and by 10.00 pm. on weekends.

With my first weeks wage, I first handed over half of my wages to Mum, then I went to the shops and bought my first single record, which was Sonny and Cher's, 'I got you babe'. I then bought ten cigarettes, and because I

Lollipops, Bubblegum, Death and Lies

felt grown up, I 'splashed out' on a packet of Benson and Hedges, then the height of smoking luxury!. The rest was saved for my bus fare and any clothes that I needed, so not bad going for a weekly wage of £4.17s 6d!.

One Saturday, I was lazing about in bed, when I heard noises coming from Mums bedroom, Oh my God, she and Maurice were 'at it'!. I felt sick at the thought, not so much because she was having sex, but, for goodness sake, my Dad had only been dead five months!. Couldn't she have waited just a little bit longer?. I didn't know whether to pretend to still be asleep, or get up and dressed, so I decided to stay where I was 'till I heard them get up and go down stairs. I wasn't ready to face them yet, as I still felt embarrassment at what I'd heard. Not long after that I heard a knock on my bedroom door. I quickly lay back down, turned to face the wall, and closed my eyes. It was Maurice who called my name, and said 'cup of tea', and I turned over to see him standing there with the cup and saucer in his hand. He was wearing my Dad's brown shirt, open at the neck, with bracers over the top holding my Dad's trousers up, and my Dad's slippers!.

How could she, how could my Mum allow

Maurice to wear my Dad's clothes?. If I hadn't liked the situation before, I hated it now, and inwardly I was seething. Maurice would never take the place of my Dad, and I knew, that even if they were ever to marry, I would never call him Dad. Bloody hell, only five months on, and he was sharing Mum's bed, Mum's body, and Dads clothes!. Maurice carried on sharing the best of both worlds, as Mondays and Thursdays he would spend living at his own house with his Dad and sister, and Tuesdays, Wednesdays, Fridays, and the weekends, he would be living with us.

Elwyne used to visit us without Fred, as after all, if Fred had come to our house with Elwyne, he would have had to clap eyes on me, and heaven forbid he should want to do that!. Elwyne told me once, that she didn't like Maurice, she didn't trust him, and that he had no rights to wear Dad's clothes. I agreed with her wholeheartedly, and this could have been my opportunity to speak out, but I missed it, as usual deciding that it was far simpler to keep my thoughts to myself.

Christmas of 1965, was the first without my Dad, and I couldn't help but remember past Christmas's, such as the time he'd been to work on Christmas eve, and his workmates had bet him that he couldn't drink eight

Lollipops, Bubblegum, Death and Lies

double whisky's, so he told them that if they paid, he was game. Later, when he walked through the front door of our house, rocking backwards and forwards on his heels, Mum understandably flew into a rage, as he was covered in vomit which was in his hair and down his coat. Apparently, on the bus, on the way home, he'd felt sick, so he took off his trilby hat and 'puked' in there, then he placed the whole thing back on his head!. Mum ran a bath and told him to soak it off, and when he re-emerged, he was wearing his pyjamas. He just slumped in the armchair, unable to breathe properly, and was calling for us to open the window for some fresh air, so Mum flew to the window, thrust it wide open, and told him to jump out of it, as that way he could get plenty of fresh air!. The fact that we lived three stories high made it all the better as far as she was concerned. Dad would usually get drunk at Christmas, and whilst Mum was cursing him, he would be holding his pint and singing to her, 'Are you Lonesome tonight?', which was a song by Elvis Presley, to which Mum would 'tut', and call him a 'silly bastard'. I really missed my Dad and I wanted him back.

Christmas passed and New years Eve arrived. Mum had invited Elwyne, Fred, Pam and Lorraine to our house, and I don't know what tipped the balance, but Fred actually turned up with Elwyne and Kids. Once Pam and Lorraine were in bed, John had this idea that we should write out the alphabet on 26 pieces of paper, and the words 'Yes' and 'No' on others, thereby making a make shift 'ouija' board. Everyone in the room had been drinking and all agreed to play the game, but I never did like or agree with anything like that, so I said that I would just watch.

As the letters were placed in a circle round the table, 'Yes' at the top of the board, and 'No' placed at the bottom. Mum, Maurice, Elwyne, Fred and John all took a seat, and with their fingers on an upturned glass they started, with Mum asking, 'is there anybody there?'. Slowly, as the glass moved round and round, Mum asked, 'are you male or female?', and as the glass moved to the letters, they all, in unison said out aloud the letter that it was pointing to, as It spelt out 'MALE'. 'Can you spell out your name for us ?', asked Mum, but the glass just went round and round, so Mum asked the same question again. The 'glass' refused to spell anything out, so John asked, 'are you a good spirit ?', to which the glass then spelt out the word 'YES', and John said, 'tell us your name then'. The glass went

Lollipops, Bubblegum, Death and Lies

round and round again spelling nothing, and I think it was Elwyne who said, 'its not going to tell us', but John said, 'you're not a good spirit, you're evil aren't you?'. Then the glass pointed to 'No', but John taunted it, 'yes you are, you are evil, tell us who you are then!', and with that the glass went round and pointed to 'No' again.

Suddenly, for no reason, John stood up, and holding the stem of the glass in his hand, he raised it up in the air, shouting, 'you're evil!', and then he smashed the glass down on the table, sending splinters of glass all over the table and onto the floor. The blood seeping from John's hand landed on the table, and everyone looked horrified as John stormed out of the house and into the night, but I think we must all have been in shock, because it was five or ten minutes before we got our coats on and went out looking for him. I walked around the streets of Kingshurst until about 1.30 am, but when I eventually got back to the house, John had already returned home, and had placed a tea towel round his hand. I suppose, luckily for him, the flow of blood was slowing down, which was just as well really, as he refused to go to hospital. The incident now over, Elwyne and Fred then got Pamela and Lorraine out of bed, and despite protests from Mum, got them dressed and walked home from Kingshurst to Tile Cross. What a bloody marvelous way to start one's New year!!.

Chapter 16

PULLING TEENAGERS

I had begun to feel bad about myself, and though I never did have much self esteem, I felt worse than ever, and decided that my 12st 12lbs frame had to go. I told Mum that I didn't want sandwiches for work, instead I would take two cream crackers and a hard boiled egg, which I followed with a cup of coffee and a 'fag'. For tea, I would have two cream crackers and a tomato, again, followed by a cup of coffee and a fag. I kept this up for four days and lost 10lbs in weight, so now I was on a roller, if it fell off me like that, then I would be slim in no time!. Mum, however, didn't share the same enthusiasm as me and on the fifth day, instead of the two cream crackers and a tomato, there on the plate were potatoes, vegetables and steak, with the instruction to eat it, but I played my face and said I didn't want to eat it as I was full. 'You can bloody well eat it now I have gone to the trouble of making it for you, you ungrateful bastard, now eat!', she said, and I knew that she meant it, so I reluctantly carved away at it and ate. I thought of how much she had been hurt by John, and I thought, 'I can't hurt her as well', so I just did as I was told. I was happy working at the B.S.A. but a friend of mine told me that I could earn more money than the £4.17s.6d. that I was getting there, if I went to work in the servery (staff canteen), at Marston Green Maternity hospital So In July 1966, I gave a weeks notice to B.S.A, and started work the following week at the Hospital. How long was I working there for?, One month exactly!. I hated it and I missed the B.S.A. and the people I'd left behind, and so as jobs were ten a penny back then, I went to see Mr Lloyd, and told him I hated it at the hospital. He asked when I could resume my old job, and a week later I was sitting at my old familiar desk.

Like most teenagers of today, my friend Pat and I would go on the prowl looking for members of the opposite sex. One day a car pulled up along side of us and asked where we were going, to which we replied that we were going nowhere in particular, so the lads got out of the car and started to chat to us.

Lollipops, Bubblegum, Death and Lies

The drivers name was Bob, his mates name was Jeff, and we arranged to meet them the following night at the Mountford Pub car park, and as the following evening was a Friday, it that meant that I would get to stay out until 10.00 pm.

When we met them, the next night, we all went for a quiet drink and they told us that they were from, and worked in, the Aston area, I became worried about the time and told them I had to be home by10.00pm, they both laughed, but obliged by getting me back home on time, and said they would meet us at my house the next night. Jeff walked me to the front door, but, just as he was kissing me goodnight, the front door opened, (great timing or what?), and there stood John, so I broke away from Jeff who said he'd see me the following night and left.

John, when I got into the house, started to 'take the piss', and though him asking questions wasn't so bad, when he started to be derogatory towards Jeff, I sprang to Jeff's defence. John was saying things like, 'he's as tall as you are round', 'hope you didn't do anything', (that's a good one coming from him !), and, 'What do you see in him', etc. etc. So I shouted at him to 'shut it', and ran upstairs from where I could hear the muffled sounds of John, Maurice and Mum talking and laughing, and maybe I was paranoid, as they could have been laughing at the television, but at the time I thought it was about me.

The following evening Jeff and Bob turned up, but I told them not to pick me up from the house again, though I didn't give a reason, and our relationship lasted just one more week!!.

When Jeff didn't turn up one evening, John goaded me, 'Ah, no Jeff then?, he's got another girlfriend', he taunted, but what had it got to do with him?, so I told John to, 'shut up, drop dead'!, and he started to laugh. I told John to stop laughing at me, but he still went on, 'He has you know, he's got another girlfriend', and as I stood by the sideboard, my eyes glanced upon the rubber torch that John used when reading meters in outhouses. I picked it up, and holding the ring of the torch on one of my fingers, I twirled it round and round and warned John that if he didn't shut it I would throw the torch at him. Mum and Maurice were sitting at the table by the french windows, and Mum told me to put the torch down, but John kept laughing, and Maurice was just keeping out of it. Then, I don't know who got the biggest shock, me, when the torch suddenly left my

Lollipops, Bubblegum, Death and Lies

hands and just the ring was still attached to my finger, John because the torch just missed his face, or Mum, as the torch flew past her and straight through the pane of glass in the french windows!.

I can assure you, my Mum might have been a big woman, but my God she could move when she wanted to. I was quicker than her though, because I knew what was coming my way, so I turned on my heels, ran out of the living room, and taking the stairs two by two, ran into my bedroom, slammed the door shut, and remained there with my back against the door. Mum was hammering on my door, 'you open this door, you little bastard', and when I didn't, she told me that she could wait, as she was in no hurry. My God, I though better than going downstairs again that evening!.

Next pay day, my full weeks wages were handed to Mum so that she could have the window pane replaced, and with no money left, I had to walk to work every day for the following week. I decided not to talk to John at all, as we wound each other up, him far more than me!.

As Christmas 1966 arrived, I thought back to the previous year and hoped that there would not be a repetition of the events that had taken place on the last New Years Eve. I went shopping in Birmingham for presents, where I bought an Airfix plastic model of a Werewolf for John, as he thought he would like to try his hand at model making. On Christmas day when we opened our presents, John had bought me a brown corduroy two piece suit, and Mum bought me a 'parka' coat and a pair of brown mock crocodile skin shoes. Although the coat was the wrong one, as I had actually wanted a Reefer Jacket, I was still pleased and grateful for the things that I had received. There were no signs of last years fiasco, John got on and made his model, and when it was finished he kept it on his bedroom window sill.

My 1967 New Years resolution was to lose more weight. Although I was already losing weight, I realized that I was never going to be a size 10, but even a size 14 would do for me, and I was beginning to feel good about myself. I had the customary posters on the bedroom wall, of Chris Farlow, The Yardbyrds, the Troggs, and maybe one or two of the Beatles, and I would put my music on, tie a pyjama cord to the coat hook on the back of my bedroom door and 'dance' with it!.

I had a boyfriend, Steven H, who I kept away from the house for obvious reasons, and

Lollipops, Bubblegum, Death and Lies

I was happy-ish. Steven and I would go to a youth club where we would meet our friends, although some nights I would have to meet him there. He would turn up on his Norton 750cc motorcycle, but I was never tempted to go on the back of it, as motorbikes frightened me, and still do today, so he would walk me home, pushing the heavy machine by his side. I don't know why now, but I thought Steven was too young for me, although he was only two months younger than I was, so I ended this relationship before it got going!.

I was wearing make up by this time, but I had to hide it at home, and only when I got to my friends house, would I put on the Rimmel silky beige foundation, brown lip stick and false eye lashes. The problem with those lashes was that they kept catching on my 'specs' and they would end up drooping, so I gave up on those as a non starter!. From then I started to use a mascara block. I would spit on the block and rub the brush over it, then apply the thick black gunge over my lashes, being careful not to blink, in case I ended up looking as though someone had blackened my eyes for me!. When I got home, I would have to make sure the coast was clear from John's prying eyes, as If he ever caught me wearing 'that muck', he would have pulled rank again.

In May, Mum dropped a bombshell, (she might have been having sex with Maurice, but, no she wasn't pregnant!). She was going off to Canada for the last week of July, and the first week of August, to stay with my sisters, Doreen and Jean. Mum felt that John and I were old enough to cope on our own, but panic began to set in for me, as that would be like leaving the bear in charge of the honey pot, he WOULD get to it, and devour it!. There was no way that I would want to be left for a whole fortnight with John, on my own, in that house. But how could I tell Mum about my fears, how could I tell her that I was worried that John would pester me into a shag?, after all, she had no idea of what had happened to me in the past. By now, although still quite naive about some things, I wasn't naive enough to believe that John wouldn't try it on again!.

As Mum had always woken me up for work, I began to form a plan. If I told her that I was concerned about getting up for work, and worried that because of being late for work I would get the sack, wouldn't it be easier for me to stay at Elwyne and Fred's house?. I did wonder which would be the worse of two

Lollipops, Bubblegum, Death and Lies

evils, but I reckoned that with Fred working nights, and me working days, we just might miss each other as one came in from work and the other went out. So Mum approached Elwyne and asked her if I could stay there. Elwyne said it would be OK, and although there were only two bedrooms, I could share with Pamela and Lorraine. Now my mind was put at rest, but I also had to explain to John as to why I was staying with them, so I gave him the same excuse that I had given to Mum.

A few weeks before Mum was due to fly out to Canada, John was off work with depression. I don't know the full extent of the story, but it seems that someone had reported John for 'pocketing' the money he collected from the meters on his rounds. Maurice said that John hadn't done this, and that another employee was just out to cause trouble, but I knew that John wasn't coping, and I wondered just how long it would be before the 'cry for help' came again.

One evening I was sitting at the table making a Bugatti car model kit, when I heard John come down the stairs, and as he came through the living room door, I noticed in his hand the completed werewolf model that I had bought him for Christmas. He walked over to the table and said, 'I'm not superstitious… but', and then he brought his hand down on the table with a thud, smashing the werewolf model to pieces, then he just walked out of the living room and went back into his bedroom. I asked Mum what was wrong with him, but she just shrugged and told me to leave it, and as I looked at the smashed model, I didn't know whether to leave it where it was, or scoop up the pieces and put them in the bin. I wondered if it was because of something I had done, whether it was to do with his job, or whether it was because he'd not got a girlfriend anymore. I honestly don't know, but I was really hurt to think that he had to deliberately break the first present I had ever bought him for Christmas in front of me. He could have told a white lie and said he'd had an accident with it, that it had got broken. I wondered how would he have felt, if I had held up the suit he'd brought me, and set fire to it in front of him?. I was so bewildered by his actions.

Soon, John returned to work and the truth came out. One of his work colleagues admitted starting a rumour, which had escalated, and because it had reached 'higher' offices, it had to be investigated. It put John in the clear,

Lollipops, Bubblegum, Death and Lies

but the damage had been done, and It seems Maurice had been correct.

The last week in July and Mom's holiday drew ever closer. Mum couldn't have been overly concerned about John's mental health, or perhaps she could not pick up on the signs, perhaps she simply saw the opportunity for some respite for herself, but the planned trip to Canada went ahead. I didn't go to see her off, instead I went to Elwyne and Fred's before her departure. Pamela and Lorraine couldn't contain their excitement at my stay with them. I'll give Fred his due, he didn't ignore me, although I felt the tension there, but I thought it best to keep myself to myself and spend as much time as possible with Pamela and Lorraine in their bedroom where all their toys were. Can you believe it?, I was seventeen years old and playing with 'Jacko' the monkey!!, but It had nothing to do with Michael Jackson, the pop star, as this 'Jacko' was a large toy monkey, and Pamela loved him dearly.

I tried to help out as much as I could, and didn't mind too much playing in the garden with both kids. During the first weekend there, John came to visit, and he went into the garden where Pamela and Lorraine were playing. I watched closely as John got Pamela down onto the floor and was on top her, tickling her, when suddenly Elwyne rapped on the kitchen window and shouted at John, 'That's enough Jonny, get off her!'. He jumped up, and sprang quickly to his own defence, 'I was only playing,' he said. She called Pamela into the house, and ranted at John, 'you're bigger than she is, you could have hurt her!'. It's a good thing that Fred wasn't there, and I wondered if Elwyne was truly concerned that John's weight might have been too much for Pamela to bear. It might just be that she had some suspicion that John was capable of abuse, and that the 'tickling' might have been an excuse to touch Pamela's 'bits', but I'll never know. Shortly after that incident, he went back home to Oakthorpe Drive, and it was never mentioned again.

One day, I asked Fred if he would call me for work as he came in from doing his night shift. The reply was curt, 'you don't need me to wake you up, before going to sleep, just keep saying to yourself, I need to wake up at 6.30, and you'll do it', in other words, 'get yourself up'. So, on the Sunday night I went to bed and repeated 6.30 over and over again, which worked, but only because I was so conscious of not wanting to be late for work, that I didn't get any sleep at all!.

I heard Fred come in, waited until he'd had his cigarette, and then when I heard their bedroom door open, I took my clothes into the bathroom where I dressed, washed, cleaned my teeth, put on my make up, and combed my hair, then I was out on my walk to work. I repeated the same sequence everyday for the first week.

At the weekend, I offered Elwyne some housekeeping money, but she told me she didn't want any, and to spend it on myself. She then asked if I fancied a trip to 'The Rock' (Alum Rock), as now that I had lost some weight, (I was now down to 9st l0lbs and a size 14), I should treat myself to some new clothes.

The next day, we got up early and Elwyne, Lorraine, Pamela and myself went shopping. In one of the small clothes shops I saw a green floral dress that had a long zip running down the front. My God it was short, but Elwyne encouraged me to try it on, so I slid back the curtain to the changing room, undressed and tried the dress on. I looked at the transformation in the mirror, then gingerly opened the curtain so that Elwyne could take a peek. She told me how nice it looked, but that I should buy a pair of tights to wear underneath the dress, because the flash of a stocking top in a short dress would do nothing for my decorum, so I bought my very first pair of 'suntan' tights to go with the dress. Elwyne also bought Pamela some new clothes and tights from the same shop, and I dare say Lorraine was also 'treated', though I can't remember now what she had.

When we'd had enough of shopping and had spent our hard earned cash, we caught the bus back to Elwyne and Fred's house where I sat talking to Elwyne and I told her, 'You know John will kill me for wearing a dress this short', but Elwyne said, 'If he starts, send him to me, you deserve to treat yourself and you certainly don't look 'tarty' in that dress'. I was walking on cloud nine, I felt 'Trendy', for the first time in my life, and I decided that I was going to wear it for work on Monday.

Elwyne had informed me earlier that Fred was starting his two week annual holiday, and so they were going to go for days trips out with Pam and Lorraine. She said that it was more than likely I would come home to an empty house after my day at work, but that she would give me a key to let myself in.

On the Monday morning, I got myself up, had a wash, and brushed my teeth, then, taking care not to ladder my new tights, I put them on. I then undid the zip on my dress and slid it over my head, but as I smoothed it down, I felt awkward. It hadn't felt like this in the shop when I bought it, I now felt as though I had no rights to look good, and I was still worried as to what John would say when he saw me wearing it. Well, awkward or not, I <u>was</u> going to wear it!. I left Pamela and Lorraine sleeping, and there was no sound coming from Elwyne and Fred's bedroom, so I quietly let myself out through the side door and locked it after me.

On my way to work, a car sounded it's horn, then pulled up just in front of me. I thought it was a work colleague stopping to give me a lift, so I ran up to the car, and without really looking I climbed in. Then I got the shock of my life, as there in the drivers seat was a man I had never seen before!. He was black skinned, and his white teeth glistened as he smiled at me, then he said, 'Hello der darlin', where you wanna go?'. I made my apologies, told him that I thought he was someone else I knew, and hastily got out of the car whilst still apologising profusely to him. I felt that I was lucky, as he could have turned nasty on me.

While I am writing this, I've just been thinking that perhaps he thought I was a 'lady of the night' returning home after her night shift!. I must point out that it wasn't the colour of his skin that shocked me, he could have been red with blue spots for all I cared, it was the thought of my own stupidity at getting into a car before I had checked who the driver was, which was more frightening. 'Idiot' being the word that comes to mind!.

I finished walking to work, clocked in, and took my place at the typewriter, then at break time I went to the machine to make my coffee, but I found myself blushing, as I felt eyes on me and heard 'wolf whistles'. I couldn't get back to my office quickly enough, but in truth, It felt really good, and there was no going back to skirts and dresses that came below the knee from now on. I shouldn't have worried about John having his say about the dress, after all I had Elwyne on my side if he did say anything to me, but the worry <u>was</u> still there nevertheless.

Chapter 17

JOHN FINALLY GETS HIS WISH

The 31st July, 1967, started like any other day, though I knew Elwyne, Fred, and the children were going out for the day, and that I would have to let myself into their house once I had got home from work. That evening, on my walk home, I wondered how Mum was enjoying her stay in Canada with Doreen and Jean. We had not yet received a card from her, so we had no way of knowing how her holiday was going. As I approached the house, Elwyne and Fred's alsatian dog, Kim, who was kept in a kennel outside, started to bark, so I went over and made a fuss of her. I then let her off the chain and gave her some water from the outside tap, before letting myself into the house.

All was quiet, and it was a lovely warm sunny evening. I put the kettle on ready to make myself a cup of tea, then I went to the front door and picked up the post and the Evening Newspaper and went back into the kitchen. As I sat at the table reading the Paper and waiting for the kettle to boil, Kim had started barking again. I looked up, and she carried on barking, so I thought I'd better go and see what she was barking at. As I stuck my head around the door, by the gate stood a policeman. My heart raced, and my first thought was for Elwyne, Fred, and the Kids, had they been involved in an accident?. When I asked if my sister was alright, he asked me who I was. I told him my name, Brenda Fewtrell, and that I was staying here with my sister Elwyne Beasley. The policeman then asked me how old I was, and I replied 'seventeen'. He asked me if I could put the dog in the back garden, and after I had done so I was able to let the policeman into the house.

It was then he asked me if I knew John, and I told him that he was my brother. Although he asked me to sit down, I remained standing, and asked him what John had done this time. He said, 'I'm afraid its bad news, he's had an accident'. When I asked if he was OK, the policeman shook his head, and told me, 'No, I'm sorry, he's dead'. I asked him what had happened, and he said that John had gassed

Lollipops, Bubblegum, Death and Lies

himself, at home. The full comprehension of what this young policeman was telling me couldn't have sunk in, because I told him that I was just about to make a cup of tea, and would he like one?!. Suddenly the penny dropped, my tears welled up, and I asked if I could go and see him, but he told me no, it would be better not to, because the lack of oxygen had turned his body blue. When I asked where he was, I was told that he been taken to the mortuary in Coleshill

For some reason I had to get out of the house and go,...anywhere!. I wanted to run, I wanted to be anywhere but here in this house, so I ran towards the gate. God only knows where I would have gone, but instead of carrying on, I stopped and slumped over the gate, my heart breaking. The next thing I heard was Fred's voice, and perhaps it was the only time he felt some compassion for me, as he shouted to me, 'Stay there bab!'. The policeman was by now behind me, and he informed Elwyne and Fred of the same news. John had at last been the victor in his own quest, he was dead.

I went into the house, and then into the bathroom where I cried silently, as I didn't want anyone to hear me. Shortly, there was a knock on the bathroom door and it was

Pamela's voice pleading with me to open the door. I slid the latch back, and there was poor Pam, she was ten years old and trying her best, in her childish way, to comfort me. I could still hear the soft sounds of the policeman's voice talking to Elwyne and Fred, and I walked past Pamela to the bedroom, assuring her that I was alright. I really wanted to be left alone, but I couldn't send this child away, who was only doing what she thought right, so I just lay on the bed with my face in the pillow and I sobbed.

When the policeman had left, Elwyne came into the bedroom and asked me if I was alright. I nodded my head, and asked her if she knew that John was in Coleshill Mortuary, and she said that the policeman had told her all she needed to know. My opportunity had come yet again to tell her what had happened to me with John, but I knew this wasn't the right time, and I couldn't bring myself to tell her. Instead I half-heartedly tried to joke that I would no longer have to worry about what John was going to say about 'the dress' after all.

Poor Pamela, she was just a child, and I don't think that she fully understood life, let alone death. Yes, she knew that both Elwyne and I were upset, and she knew that John was dead. I don't know if Elwyne told her, at that time, the circumstances surrounding his death, and really, being a child, did she have any need to know?.

Life goes on, as I knew only too well, and Elwyne contacted Mum in Canada to tell her about John. There was no point in me staying at home the following day, so I went into work and in passing informed my work colleagues of my brothers death, then got on with my days work. I wanted sympathy from no one, my mind was in turmoil, and I selfishly thought, 'thank God it's over for me!', I would no longer have to worry over his attempts to hurt me sexually or mentally. Thank God this is last time he will put Mum through any trauma when he decides the time has come again for him to take yet another overdose. I hated him, how could he put Mum through all this shit again. I loved him because he was my brother, but how could I thank God for releasing me, knowing that Mum would be devastated. God forgive me, I actually felt an inner happiness and a great relief, but I knew that I could never explain or show my feeling.

Chapter 18

SOME CLOSURES

Saturday 3rd August was the earliest flight back from Canada, and Elwyne and I walked into the house at Oakthorpe Drive, to find that Mum hadn't long arrived home herself. I asked Mum if she was OK, though I could see she'd been crying, and she told me she'd had a lovely holiday. Then, quite out of the blue, she rolled up her sleeve and asked if we liked her suntan. Elwyne exclaimed, 'For God's sake Mum, your son has just died and you're going on about a bloody sun tan!'. I left them to their 'words', and I went upstairs where I gingerly pushed open John's bedroom door.

It was strange, his bed had been made, and as I breathed in I could 'smell' him, a kind of musty smell, but not a dirty one. What went through my mind as I scanned the room whilst listening to the argument going on down stairs, was a mixture of sibling

Lollipops, Bubblegum, Death and Lies

love and a passionate hate for him. Again, I couldn't let myself believe that he was gone, that I was never going to see him again, that I would not have the worry of him touching me, or of me having to touch him, or of him having his way with me. I would not have to protest anymore, I was safe, and that 'safeness' from his advances was to last for ever more.

I heard the front door slam, so I closed John's bedroom door and walked down stairs and into the living room. Mum was sitting at the table, resting her chin on her hands, and I asked where Elwyne had gone. With a shrug of her shoulders she just replied, 'home'. Mum had tears in her eyes, but I could not bring myself to tell her that things would be fine, and I could not bring myself to put my arms round her. I started to feel useless that I could not comfort her, but even if I could, it wouldn't bring her son back, and it was his arms around her that she really wanted.

I later found out that it was Maurice who had found the body. John had sealed round the living room door, but not others, then placed a pillow in the grate. He had then turned on the gas tap, allowing the gas to permeate the pillow, placed his head face down onto the pillow and breathed in the gas.

His hand was apparently still stretched out towards the gas tap, and I often wondered if he was having second thoughts. Had he tried to turn off the gas, but was slipping in and out of consciousness, and never managed it?. There had been a bible found by John's side, in which a passage was underlined. It was never divulged to me what that passage read, as the bible became the property of the police, and I don't know if even Mum ever found out what it read.

Mum registered the death and made the arrangements for John's funeral, which was to be held at the same place as Dads cremation, in Perry Barr. There was an air of deja vu, as it wasn't that long ago that we were doing this for Dad.

Jean could not afford the air fare from Canada to England again so soon after Dads funeral, but Elwyne attended, though she did in fact make her own way to Perry Barr. On the day of the funeral, the flowers lay on the ground of the front garden, just as Dad's had two years previously, I also wore a black arm band, just as previously, and the chief mourner walked in front of the hearse, just as he had done before. When we reached Perry Barr crematorium, we watched as Johns coffin was carried in, with the minister walking in

Lollipops, Bubblegum, Death and Lies

front of the coffin reciting a prayer. Mum was supported by Maurice, and Mum had her arm round me, though little did she know my true feelings. I didn't need supporting, I shed the obligatory tears, and I suppose that I did somehow mean them, but I couldn't help but feel that a huge weight had been lifted from me. Elwyne, although she attended the funeral, sat at the back of the church, as after Mum's inconsiderate 'suntan' remark, Elwyne found it hard to forgive her.

After the Prayers and hymns, the deep red curtain parted to allow John's coffin through, and my emotions suddenly ran true as I cried for him, after all said and done, he was still my brother. After the funeral Me, Mum and Maurice travelled back home in the hearse, and Elwyne left the same way as she arrived, by bus. As we were travelling home, I couldn't help thinking, 'Isn't it a crime to take your own life?, isn't suicide against the law?, OK, so what is the law going to do about it?, they can't send him to the gallows, they can't lock him up and throw away the key,...so the law is a joke'. He was gone, and there was nothing that anyone could do about it.

Back at home, Mom put the kettle on, and I went upstairs and quietly listened to my records. I spent the rest of the day alone in my room, where I cried. I hated him, then I loved him, then back to hating him again!. When I eventually went downstairs, my eyes were red and puffy, but nothing was said, Mum was drinking a cup of tea and staring out of the window, and Maurice was sitting opposite her. I wanted to throw my arms round Mum and tell her everything would be OK, and I wanted to tell her that John hadn't been a bad son, but to me, that would have been a lie, after all he'd really hurt Mum and Dad in the past. The mood in the house remained sombre, and that night as I lay in bed, I heard Mum and Maurice talking in whispers. I couldn't make out what was being said, but then I did hear Mum quietly sobbing, so I do hope that Maurice was comforting her, because I would have found it so hard to carry out that task. I was so sad, I loved my Mum, but had no idea how to show her, and sometimes, it takes more than a kiss or a cuddle to make things right.

After Johns death, I felt as though I had a new lease of life. I was allowed to stay out until 10.00 pm during the week, and 11.00 pm at the weekends. My friend and I started to play the game of one night stands, and we would find some unsuspecting males and let them pay for our admission to places. After

Lollipops, Bubblegum, Death and Lies

they had plied us with cigarettes and booze, my friend and I would say we were going to the loo, and then do a 'runner', never to see them again...hopefully!. As it happens, one night my friend and I went to a pub called the 'Tyburn House', and when we scanned the room, we giggled as we saw three separate groups of lads that we'd run out on previously, so needless to say we didn't hang around! Instead, we went back to her house with a bottle of cider and ten 'fags', and listened to The Beatles on her record player, as It was far simpler than dodging lads.

Unfortunately I lost track of time and ended up walking home from Castle Vale to Kingshurst, and I knew that I was going to be home much later than the ll.00 pm deadline Mum had given me. In fact, as I was walking home at around midnight, I saw a familiar Hillman Minx car go past, in which the driver was Maurice and the passenger was Mum, but because the path was off set from the road, they drove past without seeing me. I knew I was in trouble, so I ran, and instead of keeping to the main road, I took the back roads through Shard End and onto Kingshurst. I was too late, Mum and Maurice were already home, and an argument ensued, because they told me they had been out looking for me, though I didn't let on that I had seen them. The next night, I was told that because I could not be trusted to be home at a reasonable time, I was to be home by 9.30 pm, and so I was, No questions, I just did as I was told.

That Christmas,1967, was a peculiar time, no John, no Dad, no visits from Elwyne and the kids, just me, Mum and Maurice. I couldn't tell you what I had for Christmas, or what we did, if anything, for New Years Eve, and so began 1968.

My friend was still playing at one night stands, but this time she had met someone that she really liked, and so our nights of 'messing around' came to an end. I began to stay at home, alone in my bedroom, listening to my records, and leaving Mum in the company of Maurice. On the nights that Maurice didn't stay over, Mum and I would watch the programmes on the television, and talk of the days events, but she never once mentioned John or Elwyne. I felt my family loyalties torn, as I loved and respected Mum too much to betray her by visiting Elwyne, but I also loved Elwyne, she was after all my big sister, and I also loved and missed my nieces. I did what I thought was best, but not necessarily right, and I stayed away from

Elwyne's house. I can't turn the clock back, and in some respects I'm pleased that I can't, but I do wish that I hadn't ignored Elwyne and her family for so long.

Brenda, age 9

Lollipops, Bubblegum, Death and Lies

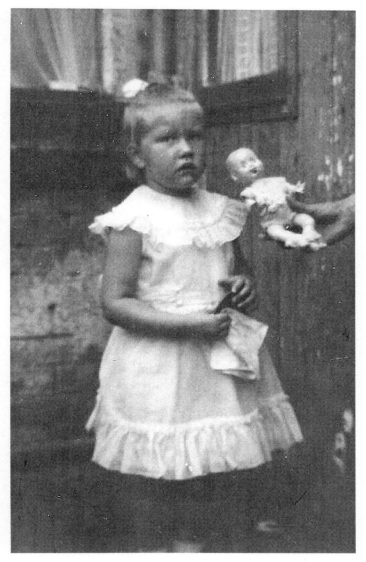

Pamela, age 3

Susan, aged 3

Lollipops, Bubblegum, Death and Lies

Susan, aged 5

Brenda and Michael ,Dunster August 1968

Lollipops, Bubblegum, Death and Lies

Michael 2009

Brenda 2010

Lollipops, Bubblegum, Death and Lies

Pamela 2008

Ginnette

Lollipops, Bubblegum, Death and Lies

Karl

Brenda Fewtrell Brown

Stephen

Chapter 19

A NEW PERSPECTIVE ON LIFE

I was still working at the B.S.A., when one lunchtime, one of the female machinists, Moira, asked if I fancied going for a drink over at the Mackadown pub, which was situated opposite the factory. It was a lovely summers day, so off we went. Over at the pub, she went to the bar and bought the drinks, then we sat talking about things in general.

After a while, she said to me, 'see him over there ?'. I looked round to see a young Tommy Steele look alike sitting with two of his female work colleagues, 'Well, He plays the drums'. She told me that she used to deliver the newspapers to his house some time back, before she had left school. As he walked past us on his way to the bar, Moira called over to him, 'Ello Mick!'. He looked around, then walked over to where we were sitting. Moira then asked him, 'where are you working now?', and he replied, 'James Booth Aluminium, in the Export department offices'. Unfortunately, on hearing that, the very first thing I said to him, almost in a subdued voice was, 'No wonder the country is going to the dogs!'. Moira then introduced me, 'This is Brenda', and I smiled at him, this time without saying anything!. Then Moira added, 'You'll want to be careful of her, she'll have your trousers off before you can blink!'. God only knows why she said that!. I could feel the embarrassment rising in my face, and I kicked her playfully under the table. She just laughed.

The following Friday, Mick was in the Mackadown again. He made a point of coming over to the table we were sitting at, and we chatted, passing the time of day over our lunch time drinks. Before he went, he put his hand on my back and said to me, 'There's a film on at the Scala cinema called 'Doctor Zhivago', be ready for 6.30pm if you want to come', (And who said romance was dead?), he then asked where I lived, and I told him my address. He turned up (late!) in his Ford Anglia and drove into Birmingham, and although he paid for me, he didn't hold my hand, but asked me to slip my arm through his,...Aahh!!. The film was actually a love story set around the time of

Lollipops, Bubblegum, Death and Lies

the Russian revolution, in the early twentieth century, and 'whoosh',... it went straight over my head. I've since watched that film again three times before I could finally understand and appreciate it.

Once home, Mick pecked me on the cheek and asked if I would see him again. Although I really had no intention of seeing him again, I told him yes, so he said that he would see me on Monday night and left. I'd had a nice evening, and he wasn't bad company, he'd got a car, he'd paid for me to get into the cinema, so what was my problem?. It was simply because I didn't feel ready for a relationship, and I was happy having occasional one night stands. So, when Monday arrived, and I heard the door knock, I asked Mum if she would tell Mick that I had already gone out. Mum told me to 'do my own dirty work', so I answered the door with a smile on my face, invited him in, and we spent the evening at my house.

We had been going out for some weeks, and I knew that Mick had a failed engagement behind him, but he didn't talk about her very often. One night, we went for a drink at The White Hart pub, in Tile Cross, when he saw some people that he knew, and we walked over to where they were sitting. They asked us to join them, and Mick introduced me to them. One couple was a lot older than the other, but we talked, I felt relaxed in their company, and we generally had an enjoyable evening. We left after making arrangements to meet the younger couple on the Friday.

One our way home I asked Mick if he worked with them, and he told me no, they were his ex-fiance's Mum and Dad, and her sister and her boyfriend. I was totally stunned, to think I could have mentioned his ex and really slagged her off, not realising who these people were!. I was so annoyed with him for not being truthful with me, and to make matters worse, we were going out with his ex's sister and her boyfriend again the next Friday!.

I should have told Mick there and then that he could stuff this game 'up his jacksie', but I didn't. In fact, over time, I became quite good friends with this couple, Dave and Pauline, so much so, that when they married, we went on their honeymoon with them!. To explain however, this was only for a few days, and only because they missed their train to Barmouth, in Wales, so Mick ended up taking them there in his car!.

Mick and I made a lot of friends in the Rowley Regis area near Dudley, in the 'Black country', where Dave and Pauline lived.

Every Friday evening he would pick me up from my house, and we would go over to The 'Brick house' pub and meet them. I still fondly remember our friends Trevor and Madelaine, and Bob and Alice, who we would see regularly. It was such a good time in my life.

When the time came for the inevitable to happen (sex!) with Michael, he didn't want to force me into anything I wasn't ready for. He let me be in total control, and although I held back my true feelings, I didn't feel this was wrong. It wasn't like the sex I had known with John, this was more than sex, this was gentle, this was right, this was love and not just lust.

One of the one places that we used to drive out to, that I totally fell in love with, was the ancestral Home of the Shirley Family. This mansion was on the far side of Stratford upon Avon from where we both lived, and was known by then as Ettington Park Hotel. It was owned at the time by a lovely old Gentleman, Mr.Shaw and his family. I felt so privileged when Michael and I walked into this grand, quiet place, and Mr Shaw would walk up to us, shake our hands vigorously, and always greet us with the same words, 'Well, I'll be jiggered!, how are you both?'. We would be invited to sit down, and we would buy a drink in the library bar where Mr Shaw would join us. He would tell us the history of the place, and how his children had been baptized in the attached 12th century chapel.

He held the place on a ninety-nine year lease, but his only son, whom I believe was in the R.A.F, had no interest in the place. Mr Shaw was always saddened by that because he knew that the time would eventually come when he would have to leave the place to someone new. One thing he would often tell us was that if you wanted to teach a child patience, then let that child have horse riding lessons, but I knew that this, for us, was out of the equation, as that past time was only in the reach of 'monied' peoples.

Mr Shaw was so proud of Ettington, and he would tell us many anecdotes about his time there. One such story was how he'd had a large marble sculpture of a Lady in a Dutch Bonnet stolen from the grounds. The police eventually tracked it down to a dealer who had brought it from some teenagers who'd visited Ettington one day, and on their way out had decided to 'nick' it. They had sold it to him for £40.00p, but the dealer knew that this item was worth a lot more than that, and had marked it up at £400.00p. After that

Lollipops, Bubblegum, Death and Lies

incident, Mr Shaw decided to have it insured for over £800.00p, which was a lot of money even then.

Another story he related to us, was of a frog that had somehow got buried alive in the foundations of the house. Although I've no idea why the frog (or was it a toad?) should have been buried originally, It was only found and released many years later, when building alterations were taking place. He would tell us that it was his wife, who was really the business woman, and about his children and grandchildren. His two dogs, a 'Harlequin' Great dane, and a rather large dalmation would always be there, either waiting to be made a fuss of, or lying in front of the enormous heraldic fireplace in the hall. He was a true gentleman, and always said how much he enjoyed seeing Michael and I for a chat.

One of the many interesting tales that I remember well, was about Jan (Yan), His barman, who had come over from Poland to England during the second world war. He had lost all contact with his wife and family in the meantime, and feared that they had perished during the war years. After a number of years he went on to marry another Polish woman who had also made her home in England, however, the long and short of this story is that his first wife was actually still alive, and many years later had managed to trace and contact him!. It was all eventually sorted out amicably, and the two Polish women developed a firm bond of friendship, to the extent of even exchanging knitting patterns and recipes between Poland and England for many years!.

Chapter 20

MR AND MRS

One year after we met, Michael and I became engaged, then a year after that we put plans in motion for our marriage. The wedding was to take place at Kingshurst Methodist church on 21st November 1970, and the reception was to be held at The Digby Hotel, Water Orton. I asked Stan to give me away, and although it was a tentative relationship, Elwyne, Fred, Pam and Lorraine had made up their differences with Mum, so I asked Elwyne if Pamela and Lorraine could be our bridesmaids.

Money was tight, and I knew that my Mum would not be able to afford the marriage costs, so Michael and I started to save like mad for our wedding. When I eventually went into Birmingham to buy my wedding dress, the whole outfit, wedding dress, veil and shoes came to £33.00, it was a lot of money to us, as my wage at this time was £10.14s 6d. (£10.75p). Because we were paying for our own wedding, we did without a professional photographer, and instead of flowers, I was going to carry a small white bible. David, who was Michael's youngest sister, Melodie's boyfriend, was a chef, and he made the wedding cake for us, and because Disco's were still a new thing, and expensive, we provided our own ,...... well, someone provided a record player, and someone else provided the vinyl records!. Our buffet was to cost 7/6d (35p) per head, which was, for the time, middle of the range catering cost. Eventually everything was organised,... we hoped!!.

The morning of the wedding, Elwyne, Pam and Lorraine came to our house in Oakthorpe Drive. The carnations for the button holes had arrived, a bottle of sherry had been opened,... and I was still in bed!. No rush, it was MY wedding day, MY last day of freedom, so I was staying put in MY bed until I felt that it was time to get up. I strongly believed that I should walk down the aisle as God made me, so I wore no make up, and I did my own hair, hence the reason for me not having to rush about like the proverbial 'blue-assed fly'. Stan, Marie and Lourdes arrived, so I thought

Lollipops, Bubblegum, Death and Lies

it was time I got up, especially since I was called a lazy bugger by Elwyne!.

Mum made us all a sandwich and cups of tea, and after eating I went into the bathroom and tried to make something decent of myself. Though still only half dressed, I then went into the bedroom, and Elwyne asked if I was going to wear a bit of make up. When I told her no, to say that she made no effort to hide her surprise would be an understatement!. We got on with the dressing process, with Pamela, Lorraine, Elwyne and myself all in the same bedroom getting ready. Elwyne had made Pamela's and Lorraine's bridesmaids dresses, and although the dresses were just a plain light blue, they looked lovely on the girls. I was helped into my wedding dress by Elwyne, who then placed the veil and head dress on my head. Lastly I put on my white satin sling back shoes to complete the outfit, and Elwyne complimented me on how nice I looked.

As I went downstairs, I kept thinking that my Dad should see this day, and that he should be the one 'giving me away', despite this, I was honoured that Stan had agreed to perform that duty. When everyone had left for the church and there was just Stan and I still in the house, he told me how nice

I looked, then his words of wisdom were, 'today the girl, tomorrow the woman', and he kissed me on my cheek. I picked up the small bible I was going to carry down the aisle with me, and Stan and I made our way into the wedding car waiting outside.

The church, Kingshurst Methodist, was literally a two minute walk from our house, and it took the car carrying us about thirty seconds to get there, hardly worth even switching on the ignition really!.

As Stan and I got out of the car, I slipped my arm through his, and to the sound of the organ playing 'The Wedding March', we walked down the aisle, to where Michael, and Dave, his Best man, stood at the altar. Michael was wearing the dress uniform of the Royal Army Medical Corps, as he was in the Territorial Army, and so had the rights to wear his uniform, and he had scrubbed up quite well really!.

The church was packed with our guests, and though there were only nine relatives from my side, there were more than fifty from Michael's side, and that was without our friends and acquaintances!. The marriage vows were taken, first by Michael and then by myself, but then there was an audible gasp from behind me when I made the promise to

LOVE, HONOUR AND <u>OBEY</u>, (what!, OBEY... yeah right!). We were then pronounced Husband and Wife, and I had now made the transition from Brenda Fewtrell to a 'common garden' Brenda Brown. The only thing left to do now was to sign the register, with my Mum and Michaels Dad as our witnesses. Signing the register was for us a fairly quick affair, because as I have already mentioned, we did not have a professional photographer, so no formal photographs were taken in the church.

I had walked into the church as a 'Miss' and I came out as a 'Mrs', too late to back out now! We stood outside the church whilst family and friends took photographs, and both of us felt that the ceremony couldn't have gone better. For a late November day, it was bright and sunny, and the air was crisp, everything was on time, and all the people we had invited had attended. After the photographs had been taken, some instant ones, using the 'latest' polaroid camera, we climbed back into the Daimler wedding car and off we went ,on a slightly longer ride this time, to the Digby Hotel for our reception.

We mingled with the guests, and I was given lots of good advice by well wishers, such as, 'If you do throw the ring back at him, throw it where you can find it!', and 'if he doesn't do what you ask of him, withhold sex for a month, that should see you get your own way!'. I was also told to, 'never tell him the true price of things, that way you get to keep any money that is left over!'. All well meaning advice, but none of it ever taken!. I suppose that Michael was also given some manly advice from his uncles, but he never told me of it.

The reception and buffet went very well, but the only fly in the ointment was Fred. He had got a 'bee in his bonnet' over some money that Stan owed him, and Fred decided that our wedding reception was the right time and place to make a song and dance over it. Fuelled by Fred's drinking, the argument got so bad, that Michael's uncles soon decided to intervene. Enough was enough, so all of them hoisted Fred shoulder high, on his back, with his arms and legs flailing up in the air, and with a great deal of jollity carried him downstairs, where they threw him out into the frosty night!. Of course, Pamela and Elwyne were upset, but Michael's family supported them, and with Fred not daring to show his face again the remainder of the evening went very well,

At approximately 9.30 pm, Michael and I

Lollipops, Bubblegum, Death and Lies

went back to his parents house nearby to get changed into our 'going away' clothes. There was no time for 'nookie', as we had to go back to the reception to say our 'thank you's' and goodbyes to our guests. The guests were all convinced that we were going straight to Dunster Beach, near Minehead, in Somerset that night, to Michael's Mum and Dad's chalet for our short honeymoon, but Michael had kept a closely guarded secret as he didn't want any pranks played on us,...spoil sport!. We told only my Mum, and Michaels Mum and Dad, that we were going to spend the first night in a Hotel in Evesham, Worcestershire. We had decided that it would be best not to make such a long journey on our wedding night, and on the Sunday we would travel onto The 'Ship inn' at Porlock Weir, where we would stay for four days, as that was as far as our savings would take us.

We eventually arrived at Evesham at 11.45pm, just before they locked up. It was so cold that night, that once I had changed into my 'baby doll' nighty, I jumped straight into bed,... bloody hell, that was freezing too!. Michael got into bed and we snuggled up, and though I don't need elaborate on the details of our wedding night, we knew then that we wanted to start a family, so no precautions were taken. Later, when I went into the bathroom for a wash, there, hanging on the back of the door were two hot water bottles. Oh bliss!, I filled them with hot water from the tap, and although not boiling hot, they were warm enough for some extra comfort.

The following morning, we had breakfast, and packed our clothes away. Then we paid our bill, under the names of Fewtrell and Brown, (Michael had forgotten to omit my maiden name when booking the hotel !), and started on our journey to Porlock, in Somerset.

The Ship Inn was a lovely picturesque old building, dating back four hundred years, or more, and situated facing the small harbour. When Michael had booked the hotel, he had asked for a double room on the front of the Inn, but was told that all the doubles were situated at the rear. So, no sea view for us it seemed. Imagine our surprise therefore when we checked in, to be shown to a front room, complete with sea view!. The staff had gone to the trouble of pushing the rooms two single beds together and securing them with double sheets and blankets. Sugared almonds had been placed in an oval dish on the bedside cabinet, and a radiator warmed the room, which for us, was sheer luxury.

When we looked out of our bedroom window, we could see the shore, and each afternoon before it became dark, I would sit in the little window seat and just watch the sea.

We would drive up the Porlock toll road and over Exmoor, then on to the Doone Valley, from where we travelled into Lynton and Lynmouth. We enjoyed the evenings having drinks at the Blue ball inn, on Countisbury hill, or Culbone stables on Exmoor, and of course in the Ship inn itself. Some nights, we even had nookie, in fact every night we had nookie!. On the Thursday, After a wonderfully happy few days, we reluctantly left Porlock to continue our married life at home.

In Church Road, Sheldon, We had secured a 'private' flat, that had two bedrooms, a bathroom, living room and kitchen. I had no washing machine, so my washing was done by hand in the sink, and sheets were put into the bath and scrubbed. I also had no fridge, so our bottles of milk were put into a bucket of cold water and placed in the larder. Food was bought fresh on my way to work, and then cooked when I got home in the evening, and there was no central heating, and no gas supply, so we were all electric. We did have an electric fire that had three bars, one of which was broken, and we were given my

Mums old double bed, and my old single bed, which went into the spare bedroom along with my old wardrobe. My chest of drawers, and Michael's wardrobe was kept in our bedroom.

We had bought a new settee, and table and chairs for the living room, but our carpet didn't fit wall to wall, so I polished the black tiles around the edge of the room, which was a bit dangerous, because it made the floor very slippery, but they looked all shiny and clean when I had finished with them. Those tiles eventually became so slippy that even the 'silverfish' that lived in the dry cement and ventured out in the dark couldn't scurry away quickly enough, before I caught them on some sellotape and disposed of them!. How many young couples of today would start their married life like that, eh?.

On our bed, we had the famous Brentford nylon sheets and pillow cases, which would make our hair would stand up on end when we got out of bed the following morning, and the enthusiasm for making love was often short lived, as the sheets would build up static electricity and give you a tingle over your body. This effect was nothing at all to do with passion, this was the revenge of those damned nylon sheets!. On top of the sheets, were placed blankets, and on top of that there was a 'candlewick' bedspread, as the word 'Duvet' was not even part of our vocabulary back then. The whole lot was tucked under the mattress before we got into bed, so making us nice and snug. When it was necessary to have a hot water bottle, we made use of glass pop bottles covered with an old sock!. I wonder, can you still get glass pop bottles these days?.

Michael, by this time was working for Multi-Broadcast, a television rental company, which meant that most Saturdays he had to go to work, but on the Saturday that he had off we would go to the shops on the Coventry Road in Sheldon, to Waitrose or the Co Operative store and do the shopping for the Sunday dinner. However, if Michael picked up a chicken for 10 shillings (10s=50p), I would have to remind him that we were not living in the lap of luxury, and to put it back and get one for 7/6d (= 35p!). We just had enough money left to buy some potatoes and a couple of tins of peas. All the way to the checkout, I would be chuckling and ribbing him, saying '10 bob for a chicken, I can't believe it, do you think Rockafella is your middle name?'.

Our first Christmas was a quiet affair, with just Michael and me, a bottle of sherry and a bottle of ginger wine, our roast turkey, and a Christmas cake. On Boxing day we went to my Mums for dinner, and on that evening, Michael had a 'booking', playing drums in a band, so I went along with him and sat behind the curtain back stage whilst Michael played 'til midnight. By the time we got back home, both television channels had closed down, so we just went to bed. That was it, Christmas was over. He had yet another booking on New years eve, and I accompanied him to the club he was working at. Once again I sat behind the curtain, backstage, on my own and waited for him to finish the evening. By the time we got home, it was even later than the previous occasion, and television had again closed down, so off to bed we went,… from where we emerged in 1971.

Chapter 21

EMPTY HANDED, BROKEN HEARTED

In 1971, the coal miners went on strike over pay and conditions, and the country was plagued by random blackouts. By the time we got home from work there was usually just enough time for us to have a cup of tea and a bite to eat, before the electricity would go off and we were plunged into darkness. We had no television to watch, and only candles for light, and the two remaining bars on our electric fire would quickly fade as it's life was temporarily snuffed out. God, it was freezing in that small flat, but these episodes gave us the perfect excuse to go to bed early. Good Lord, we'd only been married two months, as if we needed an excuse, but it did keep us warm!.

By the end of that January, I noticed that I had missed a period, and because of this

I gave up smoking straight away, as I was hoping that I was pregnant. I'd start each day with a good bout of sickness, but life had to go on, and I couldn't afford to have time away from work, so I'd force myself to eat breakfast before going off to work. Once there, my mind was taken off the way I was feeling and my body settled down. I was in ecstasy!. I was married and I was sure I was pregnant, and at last, I was to get what I wanted, Motherhood.

I missed three periods before I decided to make my appointment at the doctors. When I went to see him, he sent me behind a screen with the instructions to take off my bra and tights. I did just that, just my bra and tights, not my 'drawers'!, then I climbed onto the bed and he examined my boobs. He then asked me to bend my knees as he was going to give me an internal examination. He put on his latex gloves, but then stopped what he was doing, and asked me how on earth I expected him to examine me when I was still wearing my pants!. I don't know who was more embarrassed, him or me.

Anyway, the confirmation was made, he took out a calculation dial and worked out that I should give birth on the 14th October 1971, then told me that I would be hearing from the hospital in due course. I practically skipped home, but there was no big song and dance made, it was just a matter of a natural process that I was pregnant. When Michael came home later that day and I told him the news, he hugged me, as this was the wanted result of the act of our love making. As my morning sickness continued, Michael, naive, sarcastic, insensitive bugger that he could occasionally be, told me that it was all in my mind. 'Just get a cup of tea and a biscuit down you, and that will settle it'. I could have cheerfully slapped him one at times!.

I kept all of my hospital appointments and carried on working, but one day, about five months into the pregnancy, I went to work as usual, but I'd suffered a headache all day, and couldn't wait to get back into my own house where I would be able to relax. I caught the bus home, and as soon as I opened the front door, I had to dash for the loo. Once in there I was sick, and I noticed blood of a dark brownish colour mixed in with the vomit, so when I told Michael about it, he suggested that it may be best to go to the doctors the next day.

The next morning, I asked at work if I would be able to leave slightly earlier as I had a doctors appointment, though I didn't explain why. So that afternoon, I got off the bus two stops before my normal dropping off point, and I went in to see the Doctor. I explained about the blood, and he told me to get on the bed where he examined my tummy, and though he said that there was nothing to worry about, he didn't even listen to the baby's heart beat. I wasn't really convinced by his blase diagnosis, but he was a doctor and I had to trust that he knew best. I went home, and until I was to be seen at the next hospital appointment, I put it to the back of my mind, convincing myself that all would be OK.

Like thousands of other pregnant women, I was holding down a job and keeping house, so Michael suggested that I might be best to finish work in the August. I continued to go to the Ante-natal clinic and joined Ante-natal classes, where we were offered advice on things like breast and bottle feeding, sex after giving birth, how to bath a baby (using a doll), and different ways of folding a terry towelling nappy, as well as many other things. The time went quickly, and our baby played football with my rib cage, and danced on my bladder, which made me want to pee more often,...and my boobs became even bigger!. I was always assured that things were developing nicely

Lollipops, Bubblegum, Death and Lies

and as they should be. Their only concern was that, although I was putting on weight, my girth had only gone up to 38", which made the medical staff think that the baby would be very small.

Each visit, I was asked if I was sure that I had my dates right, and every time I assured them that I had. The 14th October eventually came...and went, I'd had no aches and pains, and I felt as fit as a fiddle, so when I next went to the hospital, I was told that they would put my expected confinement dates back by six weeks, but that if I hadn't gone into labour by the 28th October, then I would be induced. On Sunday 24th October, I felt a weird sensation inwardly, as the baby was very still but my tummy kept going hard. On Monday it was the same, but I didn't know why the baby had gone quiet, as I just thought it was getting ready for the birth.

On the Tuesday I attended the ante-natal class, where I spoke to the midwife who ran the classes, and explained to her about the hardening of my tummy, and the lack of any movement from the baby since Sunday. She advised me that it would be better for me to do the relaxation first, and then she would examine me, so when the health visitor took over the class, the Midwife called myself and a student nurse into a side room, where I was told to lay on the couch and lift my dress up. The midwife put the listening 'trumpet' on my tummy and listened carefully, then called the student over, and she too listened. As they started to talk over me in lowered voices, deep down I somehow knew what had happened, and tears filled my eyes. I tried to be strong and not let go of my emotions, then the midwife spoke to me again, and told me not to take any notice of what they were discussing, as it was purely medical talk. I was told that I should go to Solihull hospital straight away, (that was the confirmation of my fears, to me), and asked if I could get in touch with Michael. I phoned him up at work to tell him that I had to go to the hospital, but I asked him to pick me up from home first, as I needed to get my hospital 'stay' things.

Walking home from ante-natal class was a complete blur, and as I put my key in the front door, I just broke down and cried to God, 'Please don't take our baby, please let everything be alright!', even though I knew my prayer was going to fall on deaf ears. I soon heard Michael's key go into the lock and I tried to keep it together when I saw him, but I had to tell him that **I** thought the baby had died. Although he was visibly upset, he cuddled me, then with tears in his own eyes, we made haste to the hospital. All the way from Sheldon to Solihull, I silently prayed that I would do anything the good Lord wanted me to for the sake of our baby, and I cradled my tummy, stroking it as if to comfort my baby. Nine months I had waited, nine months of growing attached mentally, and for the last five months I had felt it moving.

Once we were at the Hospital, I told the receptionist that I had been advised to attend by the midwife at my ante-natal class. A nurse came straight away and led me to small room, where she also listened with the 'trumpet'. She pushed really hard trying to hear the baby's heart beat, but then she lifted her head, put her hand on my shoulder and said, 'I'm sorry, I think your baby is dead, and I need you to see a doctor'. She left the quietness of the room to Michael and I. and my heart was pounding, 'No, I need this baby, it's mine!', I sobbed, 'why, why?'. Very shortly an Indian doctor came in to see me, he too listened for a heart beat then told me, 'It is possible that the baby is lying behind the placenta, and the heartbeat is difficult to detect, but I think you know, don't you?'. I just nodded. The nurse then asked the doctor if she should prepare me for an induction, and I remember him saying to her, 'I don't think so just yet, look at the state of her'.

Michael and I were left alone together in that small room to grieve. I just lay on the bed and I felt the tears trickle back towards my ears, whilst Michael was sitting quietly holding my hand. We didn't need to say anything to each other, each knew what the other was going through, and besides, I was too upset to talk. When the nurse came back into the room, she told me that I was to remain lying down as I was now going to be taken to the labour ward, and once there, I was put into my own pyjamas and told to get back into bed. Michael came with me onto the labour ward, and saw me settled in, but then he had to go back into work. He assured me that he'd be up to see me later that evening, then he kissed me and left.

I lay down in the bed and hugged the unborn baby that was lying in my tummy, and I cried my silent tears, just as I have done so many times before. I kept wondering what I had done, where I had gone wrong in the pregnancy, and then it hit me, this must be pay back time for Susan's death. I cried again then, asking Susan for forgiveness, asking God to forgive me, and I wanted the world to go away, but I also desperately wanted my baby, who had not done anything to deserve this. Soon a nurse came in, so I hurriedly wiped away my tears, and she gave me two yellow and two white tablets, though I had no idea what they were for. By the time Michael came up to see me, I was drifting in and out of sleep, and I remember him making small talk as he held my hand, but nothing more. I told him that a doctor had been round, and had said that I was to be induced the next morning 27th October,1971.

Too soon, the bell rang to alert visitors that it was time for them to leave, and once Michael had left, I settled down. At 10pm a nurse woke me up to give me more yellow tablets, (why do they do that?,...wake you up to give you tablets to help you sleep!). I was soon drifting in and out of sleep again, but by 11.00pm, I had to get up to go to the toilet, as my tummy felt solid. By the time I got back into bed, the pain had subsided, but some time later, I had the same sensation of my tummy going hard. Once more I went to the loo, thinking I was constipated and that I needed to go, but luckily a nurse was passing me in the corridor, and she asked if I was alright. I told her I needed to go to the loo because my tummy kept going solid, so she asked me to get back into bed and she would come and take a look at me in a few minutes. She returned wearing a pair of rubber gloves, pulled the curtains round the bed, and told me to bend my knees up. After examining me, she told me that I was not likely to go through the night before giving birth, as I was already in labour!.

I was quickly moved into the labour room, but the drugs that I had been given earlier were so strong that I had problems staying awake. When I did come to my senses, everything seemed surreal and dream like, as if this wasn't happening to me, and only every so often I would be conscious enough to realise that there were other people in the dimly lit room with me. I suddenly felt the urge to push, so I told the midwife, who I remember as being a lovely lady, who seemed to have been at least 70 years old, so she advised me to put my foot against her rib cage and push. I was worried that I would push her off balance, but she told me not to worry, because she had been delivering babies for 45 years!. I only remember giving three hard pushes, and, at 1.03am on Wednesday 27th October 1971 our little girl was born. Perhaps stupidly, I asked if she was alright and said that I wanted to see her, but the midwife came to me, stroked my head, and told me to sleep. I couldn't fight it, the strength of the tablets were the victors this time, and I fell back off to sleep.

Later that morning, I was woken up by a nurse bringing me a cup of tea that she put on the cabinet, then helped me to sit up. I asked again if I could see my baby, but she told me it was best if I didn't. She went on to explain that the placenta had stopped feeding the baby, and that she had died some days before, so although she had been a perfectly formed baby, under those circumstances, she was not a nice colour and her skin was peeling away from her. Like a fool, I accepted that explanation because I didn't want to cause a fuss. How I regret not doing so now.

Later that same day I was transferred to Brooke House, which, although it was just across the road from the main hospital, I still had to be taken to by ambulance!. Brooke house was where the new mothers went after giving birth to their babies, but even though I was put into a side room on my own, I could plainly hear the cry of the new born babies. I just wanted to go home, but the doctor told me that I would have to stay in hospital for at least six days. I couldn't understand why, as I hadn't had any stitches, I hadn't got a baby, so why not just let me go?. I felt as though I was being tormented by the cries of those new babies, and I imagined the new mums talking to each other, discussing how their labour had gone, how many 'trophy' stitches they had needed, and what they had named their new baby. I imagined how their husbands had brought them huge bouquets of flowers, how they would be 'cooing' over their new baby, or how proud the new grandparents were going to be. It would be baby this and baby that, and I really envied them. Their nine months of waiting had been rewarded.

When Michael came to see me, I could tell he had been crying, and he told me that he had been to discuss what would happen next. The accepted practice for the hospital in those days was for them to register the death, and then to make funeral arrangements for our baby on our behalf. The baby would then be placed in a coffin, usually alongside an older person, and given either a burial or cremation service. Michael had been to deal with the relevant documents, amongst which was a 'Disposal Form', and he had got upset to think that our baby would now be thought of as nothing more than a piece of unnecessary rubbish !. Whether he could have realistically taken any other course of action in such a stressful situation, and in our particular circumstances, we honestly will never know now. A doctor had spoken to Michael in the meanwhile, and had admitted to him that if the hospital had induced me on time, our little girl would have been born alive. As naïve young parents, we didn't think to seek advice or take matters further, and even if we could afford it, nothing would change, and nothing would bring our baby back.

How cruel is nature, and how naive was I?. Four days after the birth, my boobs were rock solid and hurting like mad. I mentioned this to the nurse, who examined my boobs, and told me that milk was coming through,... Milk?, milk?, but I didn't have a baby, so why should my body produce milk?. To me, it seemed like nature was making a mockery of me, but why?, I had no need for this creamy coloured fluid and I didn't want it. When I went for my bath my nipples oozed, and as I leaned forward to turn off the taps, the fluid plip-plopped into the bath water. I had lost my baby daughter and my mind was telling me that I shouldn't produce milk, and yet here it was, making my boobs feel like two boulders. During all the talks we had been given at ante-natal, not once was it mentioned what the effects would be on your body if you were to unfortunately lose your baby. My own cure for ridding myself of this unwanted by-product was epsom salts to be taken in water, it tasted absolutely vile, but it did the trick.

I was told that I could come home on the following Tuesday, 2nd November, so the hospital phoned Michael to tell him to bring my clothes with him when he visited. When he came with my clothes on the Monday evening, he asked me if I wanted him to dismantle the cot and put the pram away before I came home, but I told him no, to leave them where they were. My mind was in turmoil, and I was totally confused. I knew that we had lost her, but I still felt elated that I had given birth, and my mind seemed to be constantly playing tricks on me. As far as I was concerned my baby must be in intensive care, and she would be coming home, though not until some time in the near future.

On the Tuesday morning I had a bath and dressed ready for Michael to take me home, and as I was sitting on the bed, the door knocked and opened, and there stood a nurse holding a small baby dressed in blue. She then asked me if I wanted to see a baby?,.... did I feck!!. I wanted my baby, why on earth would I want to see someone else's?. I forced myself to smile, falsely, and no doubt the baby was beautiful, but it wasn't mine. Though this nurse was obviously well meaning, I wished she'd just sod off and leave me alone. As I made no attempt to move from my bed, she just stood in the doorway and tilted her arms so that a small face, eyes closed, and surrounded by a blue hood, was facing me. It was as much as I could do to say, 'ahhhh'. No doubt she thought she was doing me a favour, but she was unwittingly tormenting me with what could have been mine, and as she closed the door, I crumpled onto the bed. Once she had left, the heartless cow, I put the headphones on and listened to the radio, a song was being played by Cher, and the title was' Gypsies, Tramps and Thieves'. One line went, 'three months later I'm a girl in trouble and I haven't seen him for a while', and those words really got to me, and all I could think of was all the horrible names under the sun to call Cher!, and although it was only a song, even now I hate it and can't listen to it. Why should someone, a tart, a whore be able to conceive a child, and yet I had lost mine?, but that's exactly how I felt at the time. When Michael arrived, I thanked the staff and we left, home to our little flat in Church Road, empty handed and broken hearted.

Chapter 22

RAMPANT RABBITS TO FAMILY LIFE

Seeing the pram and cot still made up ready for it's occupant only confirmed that our daughter would not be coming home, and yet, strangely, I still could not accept that. My mind kept taunting me, telling me that my daughter was in intensive care, and that I was waiting for the day that I could bring her home from hospital as the first born in our family. That day of course, would never arrive for her, but I went to the chest of drawers and took out a baby grow, which I held it up to my cheek and rubbed along my face, and I cried and I cried. For Susan's death, and what I had done with John, I had paid the ultimate price.

I knew that sooner or later I would have to face the music and meet people who had known me throughout my pregnancy but who didn't know the results. I smiled at people like some blithering idiot when they asked what I'd had, and I simply replied, 'a little girl, but she was still born'. I would then turn round and walk away, never giving them chance to offer me their sympathies, or of seeing their embarrassment at not knowing what to say. I had become an expert in the art of seemingly not to give a damn, and yet deep, deep down my heart was breaking. It seemed to me that there was a sudden population boom, for everywhere I looked there appeared to be new born babies. It was then that I made a conscious effort to be positive, and I decided that once I had had the 'all clear' after my post natal, I was going to try for another baby.

Around that time, I heard in a news report, that a baby had been taken from it's pram whilst its mother was in a shop. I felt so sorry for her, how she must be going mad with worry, but I also thought how stupid it was of her to leave a baby unattended, and that I would never do that. The police search was intense, and there were appeals made on the television asking for the person who had taken the child to get in touch with the police, whilst the parents pleaded with who ever took the baby not to harm her. A few weeks later The baby was found safe and sound, having been well looked after, and a woman had been arrested for kidnapping the baby. After that, my sympathies went from the mother to the woman kidnapper. It transpired that she had also had a still birth a few months before I had mine, but she was also suffering from post-natal depression. That poor woman must have been so desperate, to have gone to the lengths of kidnapping, and I wonder if she was so depressed that she really did not understand the consequences of her actions. She was not jailed, but received help for her illness via the mental health system. Today, I hope she has found the happiness that she so longed for, but if she had hurt that baby in any way, I would have been the first to say, 'lock her away and throw away the key'. I am not saying that what she did was right, far from it, but that old saying, 'been there,... done that', made me sympathise with her for her own loss.

Six weeks later, I went for my post natal and was told that apart from a tilted womb, I could go ahead and try again. That evening, Michael hardly got the chance to take his coat off before being dragged into the bedroom. This lasted every night for the first month, until one night he said, 'please, not tonight love, I've got a headache!', but If he thought I was going to accept that, he was wrong, and he gracefully succumbed once I stood there 'starkers'. I felt sure that one of those times would have made me pregnant, but no, my period still arrived, and Nine months on, I still wasn't pregnant and I was getting desperate. Poor Michael was getting 'bags' under his eyes, and his manhood was withering away through constant use. Then one night when we went to bed, I said to Michael, 'Sod it!, I just can't be bothered tonight', and I could have sworn that I heard him say, under his breath, 'phew, thank God for that!'.

A month or so later I had missed one period, but I didn't want to get my hopes up, and I decided to wait until the time felt right before visiting the doctor again. Eventually, time passed and I had missed three periods, so I went to see the doctor, although this time I was seen by a locum. It was the same old routine, bra and pants off, then he examined my boobs and asked if I intended to breast feed, after which he told me that breast feeding might be problematic. He then finished his examination and confirmed that I was pregnant.

I went home and waited for Michael arrive home from work, then I very nonchalantly told him the news that the baby was due on the 7th April, 1973. I couldn't afford to get excited, as I just wanted to see this pregnancy through with the best of results,...a live baby. I religiously attended all of the ante-natal and relaxation classes again, but one time, when a doctor was examining me, he asked if I was sure of my dates, and I thought 'here we go again!'. He told me that my next appointment would be in three weeks time, but that if I was still small for my dates, I would have to go into hospital for forty eight hours, to do a twenty four hour urine collection. We spent that Christmas at home, where I put my feet up and relaxed as much as possible, and paced myself for the sake of our baby. I had not returned to work since the still birth, and had no intentions of doing so now!.

Solihull hospital had recently had a new maternity block built, where four floors now catered for the needs of pregnant women. Ward M3 was for the mums-to-be who were experiencing 'problems', M4 was for gynaecological problems, and M1 was where the labour ward was situated, but I never did find out what ward M2 was intended for. So on Friday 3rd February 1973, I went into hospital for the urine collection, where I had to piddle in a big bottle, which was then sent to Good Hope Hospital, in Sutton Coldfield. I'm not a

Lollipops, Bubblegum, Death and Lies

medical person, so I'm not sure as to why they were sent away, or what exactly the results told the medical profession. I really expected that I would be going home on the Monday, 6th February, but I couldn't have been more wrong, and I remained incarcerated in that hospital all through February, and through March!. This was apparently a precautionary measure, the reason being that, again, I was small for my dates.

Towards the end of March, I was taken onto the labour ward for an amnioscopy, where a 'periscope' type of instrument was to be inserted into the cervix. This would show the gynaecologist how much amniotic fluid was surrounding the baby, which could go some way to explain why I was so small. The tests finished, he assured me that all was fine, and was even able to tell me that my baby had got dark hair. From there I was taken back up to the ward and advised to rest for a few hours.

The following day, 26th March, I was reading a magazine whilst relaxing on my bed. Suddenly there seemed to be a lot of activity by the staff, and then the fire alarms started to sound, whereupon everyone in the whole of the hospital was told that they had to be evacuated from the hospital. At first I was sure that this was just a fire drill, but it was far more serious than that. As we all gathered on the far side of the hospital grounds, we were told that a 'code' had been sent through to the police from the IRA, to say that there was a bomb placed 'somewhere' in the hospital confines, and therefore the whole of the hospital had to be evacuated. One poor girl was still inside the hospital operating theatre, and she could not be evacuated as the doctors, midwife, and paediatric team were in the middle of a caesarean section operation!. Another young mum-to-be was already in labour, and the doctor and midwife were unusually encouraging her NOT to 'push'. The worst part in all of this was that the incubators holding precious little struggling premature babies, had to be unplugged, and then relied upon the 'backup' machines. It was a freezing cold day outside, especially since we were all in pyjama's and dressing gowns, but eventually the 'all clear' was given, and the young girl already in 'labour' was led in first. I have never seen someone be moved so quickly!. We were told later that evening, that the call had been a hoax, Some one, no doubt, wanting their fifteen minutes of fame.

Two days later, on the Tuesday 27th March,

Lollipops, Bubblegum, Death and Lies

I was in a lot of pain, but Sister Smith, the ward sister, told me that it could be a result of the amnioscopy, and that she would come and examine me. She told me that I was in labour, and that sometimes having that particular procedure could bring labour on, although I had some time to go yet. I remembered back to my first pregnancy and the 'painless' contractions I'd had, and I thought, 'this is it', not long now'. We were, by the Grace of God, going to be a family at last, and I prayed with all my heart that I would have a safe delivery, and that our baby would be born alive.

The following morning I was still on the ward, but the discomfort I was feeling was intensifying, so by 11.30am, I was given an enema and 'de-fluffed', and was then taken down to the labour room. The hospital had contacted Michael, whilst I was given an epidural, but unfortunately I was the 1-in-1000000 that it didn't work on. Michael walked in just as I was deep in labour, but he didn't hold my hand, and he didn't stroke my head either, no, he had a ring side seat at the foot of the bed watching the whole thing!. There I was, trussed up like a turkey, huffing, puffing, grunting and groaning, when the next thing I knew was that the staff had left me, and gone over to tend to Michael who had fainted because of the heat in the room!...so he says!.

Then at last, at 1.37pm our little girl was born. A beautiful, perfect little daughter, who Michael held for a minute, before they took her away to be checked over. Michael gave me a kiss, then paid me a lovely 'compliment'. He was commenting on the procedure of the episiotomy, and told me 'tough as an old leather bucket you were!. Any other husband might have praised their wife, and have said 'well done', but no not him, 'Old leather bucket indeed!,...Cheers!

We named our daughter Ginnette Larissa, she was a tiny little dot weighing in at 5lbs 6ozs. so she was little smaller than our other daughter who had been born 5lbs.12ozs. Ginnette was placed in a cot by my side, and a nurse came in and washed me, then brought in a well earned cup of tea, by which time Michael had to return to work. I was then taken back on the ward, with my little bundle in the cot at the side of me, and as I lay on the bed and looked at her, I could hardly believe she was here, and she was mine.

At first, I was very apprehensive about getting too close to her because I wanted to breast feed her, but she was so small and

Lollipops, Bubblegum, Death and Lies

my nipples were practically none existent, but I continued to try. However by four days old, her weight had dropped to 4lbs 14ozs. and I went into the bathroom and cried. I wanted to shout for someone take her from me and help her to gain weight, because I had become convinced that I was going to lose her too. I got into such a state that Sister Smith came over to me, and I explained my fears to her. She held Ginnette and asked if I was breast-feeding her, and I told her that I was desperately trying to. She asked if she could see how I was holding Ginnette, and how I was putting my nipple into her mouth. Then as I held Ginnette and was about to feed her, Sister Smith told me to start bottle feeding her. As the doctor who had originally confirmed that I was pregnant had intimated, because my nipples were 'inverted', I would probably never have succeeded in feeding her myself. She brought a bottle of SMA milk, and Ginnette sucked and took all of 3ozs of it, so Sister Smith also advised me to feed Ginnette every three hours instead of the customary four. After the fifth day, I was discharged, but Ginnette wasn't, as the doctors wanted to see if she was progressing in the right direction. They told me that when she had reached 5lbs in weight, she would be able to come home, so instead of going home myself, I stayed in hospital with her, as the thought of her being alone there was unbearable to me.

One day, as I sat in hospital, I mused over how clever Ginnette must be, she had been due to arrive on the 7th April, but was actually born on the 28th March, which was exactly 26 days after Michael's Birthday, and exactly 26 days before mine.....How clever was that!?

The 7th April arrived, and I should have been going to Michael's youngest sister, Melodie's wedding, but I would not leave Ginnette in the hospital alone, even for a few hours. Michael felt obliged to go to the Wedding, but came to see us on the evening along with two of his aunts, who 'cooed' over Ginnette, and told me what every mother wants to hear about their new born, 'how lovely she was'.

On Tuesday, 10th April,1973, despite it starting to snow periodically, I was finally allowed to bring Ginnette home. She wore a 'baby grow' and a white hooded cape, with a blanket that my mother in law had knitted for her. I went home in my maternity trousers, as I still couldn't fit into my 'normal' clothes, unlike today's youngsters, who seem to give birth and go back to their size zero straight away!. Michael took me and Ginnette home, and I placed Ginnette into her pram and covered her up. Michael then led me into the kitchen, and there, was a 'Twin-tub' washing machine. He had bought it for me whilst I was in Hospital, but had said nothing about it. What a lovely surprise, it meant no more washing by hand at last!.

Michael had to go back to work again, as there was no paternity leave in those days, so whilst Ginnette slept, I put the 'Nappisan' into a bucket, and filled the bucket with water. I then made four bottles of feed for Ginnette using the SMA powdered milk, making it into a paste, adding boiling water, then shaking the bottles to make sure all the lumps had dispersed. A friend had given us an old fridge by then, so I was able to keep three bottles in there, and keep one out ready for when Ginnette woke up, as by then the mixture would be at the right temperature for her to drink. Next I decided to put my very first load of washing in the machine, then I filled up the little plastic bath ready to 'top and tail' wash Ginnette, and made sure her clean terry towelling nappy and rubber pants were ready for her.

When Ginnette woke, I picked her up and started to undress her ready for her wash, but what I had forgotten to do was to make sure her bottle was still warm, and how she cried and screamed for her feed!. At that moment, someone knocked on the front door, and I panicked, 'Bugger,...Multi task, Multi task, come on, what do I do now?', should I put her bottle on to warm, get her in the bath and ignore the sound of knocking, or answer the door and hope it's not Jehovah's Witnesses. Perhaps I could feed her first, and then bath her?. knowing that it would take me at least half an hour to feed her, I decided to answer the door first, and found that It was my friend, Jackie, and her 18month old daughter. Ginnette was still screaming, so Jackie took her off me while I put Ginnette's bottle on to warm, Jackie wanted to feed her, so I let her do so, but Ginnette was a lazy 'sucker' (!), and she only took 2ozs in the half hour before falling asleep again. I decided that her bath time was out for this morning, so Jackie and I 'chilled out' for a while before she went home. When she had gone, I thought that it would be a golden opportunity to spin the washing and get it hung out on the line in the communal garden area. I was just about to go out of the door, when I heard a sound in the living room, it was Ginnette who had woken up again for the rest of her bottle!. Great timing, I don't think!.....two hours later I managed to get the washing hung out at last!.

Although I 'demand fed' Ginnette because of her weight, I was determined to make sure that she was secure in a routine, so I had it planned out that she would have her bath at 5.00pm, bottle feed, then to sleep in the bedroom. Her 10.00pm feed would be given to her in the bedroom, so that she would eventually know that once she was in bed, that is where she stayed,.....der!. wrong... she decided otherwise. I know that a daughter usually turns to her mother for advice, but I was determined that I would do it all by myself, also I didn't want to ask for help for fear of being labeled a 'failure'.

Although I came across as coping well, deep inside I was under a lot of pressure, as Ginnette wasn't a good sleeper, and I now began to feel that she had picked up on my fears. I still thought that if I didn't do the right thing, then this precious child of mine would be taken away from me. It was as if Ginnette had 'slipped' through God's net and he hadn't noticed, but when he did, he would take her back, as I still felt that the things I had done with John, and for my part in Susan's death, had still gone unpunished.

I hate to admit it now, but somehow I couldn't let myself get too close to Ginnette. These were my problems and I was the only one who could deal with them, yet I loved her so very, very much, she was beautiful, and remains so to this day. I had wanted a child so badly, and now that I had got the child I wanted, something still stopped me from giving my all to her. This wasn't Post natal depression, and this certainly was not Ginnettes fault.

When Ginnette was six weeks old, Michael and I went to visit my in-laws. They owned a chalet at Dunster Beach, not far from Minehead, in Somerset, and they were going down there to clean and prepare the chalet ready for the holiday season. When they asked if we would like to go there with them, we jumped at the chance, even though Ginnette was only six weeks old, as I always loved going to Dunster. The following Friday morning, bright and early, we packed the sterilizer, formula milk, bottles, nappies, pram, nappisan, milton bleach, baby clothes, a suitcase and ourselves, and somehow managed to load everything into our small Simca car.

When we arrived at Dunster beach and had settled in, Michael wrapped Ginnette

Lollipops, Bubblegum, Death and Lies

up warm in a blanket and took her over to the beach, where he introduced her to 'King Neptune', and vice-versa. After all these years, 'King Neptune' now knows all of our children and Grandchildren!!. We loved the break, and although it was hard work, not having all the mod cons, we made the most of it. We took Ginnette out for short walks in her pram, though Michael, as was normal back in the 70's, did not want to push the pram, as that was seen as woman's work. I think that he missed out really, as I loved pushing her in the pram, and because I was very protective of her, I didn't really want anyone else pushing her anyway.

Back at home, I took Ginnette to the 'welfare' each week until she was 2 months old, and although she was thriving, she was not sleeping through the night yet. The health visitor told me to try adding some 'Sister Laura's' to Ginnettes bottle. This was a 'floury' type of substance that you mixed to a paste then added to her bottle, and it was supposed to make the milk richer, so making her feel more satisfied. Oh yeah, right!, I was full of hope, and perhaps I would get the nights sleep that I so desperately needed. So I made up her bottle, added the 'Sister Laura's', and gave the mixture to Ginnette on her next feed. Almost immediately, the damn bottle teat started blocking up, and in the end I gave up and just stuck to the SMA milk. Frustration having got the better of me, I eventually threw the once-used packet of 'Sister Laura's' in the bin!.

When Ginnette reached 5 months old, we had her christened at the same church that Michael and I had married in. I had prepared a buffet earlier that morning, but we couldn't afford to buy any alcoholic 'booze' or 'plonk', so I bought extra milk for the tea and coffee,... not quite the same!. I had already picked up her christening cake the day before, and it had cost me an absolute fortune, £3.75p!.

Ginnette had progressed well, and by five months she was sitting up unaided, but still not sleeping through the night. At nine months old she was crawling, but still not sleeping through, and by 15 months she was reciting nursery rhymes, but still not sleeping through. Soon she started to walk and getting into all sorts of mischief, but she was still not sleeping through, and, just for good measure, I had become pregnant again!!.

Chapter 23

SAME OLD, SAME OLD

This baby was due in October 1974, and once again I went to Solihull Hospital for my ante-natal. I was lucky that I had a close friend in Jackie, as she used to look after Ginnette whilst I went to the hospital. The hospital told me that the baby was growing well, but to make sure that I progressed healthily, I was to rest more during the day, or I would have to be admitted into hospital because of my past pregnancy problems. Needless to say, I assured them that I would rest.

During the afternoons, I would read a story to Ginnette, then we would both curl up on the settee for a nap. I would close my eyes and squint at Ginnette to see if she was doing the same, but of course, she wasn't. Then I would feel a little finger wend it's way up my nose, or into my mouth, so I would try to 'shush' her up, and try again, but she seemed to have a fascination for my nose, as her finger would go up there again and again. When we told Ginnette that she was going to have a baby brother or baby sister, and that the baby was lying in Mummy's tummy, she would try to look down into my belly button to see if she could see the baby!. I had to lie to the hospital staff and I told them that resting at home posed no problem at all, but with the pregnancy going well, I felt happy knowing that when this baby arrived, whether it was a girl or boy, our family would be complete.

Michael had changed his job by this time, and was now working for the Warwickshire Police force, at Solihull Police Station, but whatever his job, there was still no paternity leave. He was working hard, plus playing in a band at the weekends, and he was also still in the Territorial Army, which he had joined before we were married. One evening, after coming home from the T.A. base at Dawberryfields road, in Kingsheath, Birmingham, he told me that there was a way of earning a few extra, badly needed pounds. It meant that he would have to go away with the T.A to Aldershot, in Hampshire, and work for a couple of weeks at an army hospital, so because Michael was still low paid, we decided that it would be financially beneficial to us for him to go. I knew that there would be other females there, but I trusted him, as after all, isn't marriage based on trust?.

I still had the fear of being undeserving of yet another baby, but I could not tell anyone why I felt that way, and It worried me that I would not feel a bond with this new baby either. Then I worried that Ginnette would feel pushed out, and that I would not have enough time to devote to Ginnette, Michael, and the new baby, plus keep a house. I knew that I just had to carry on, that I had to be a good mother, and that I didn't need to rely upon anyone else. I was fairly sure that whatever happened I would cope, just as I had so many times before.

When I attended my ante-natal appointment on Friday 25th October,1974, I was asked a series of questions, then I told them that I was worried about another still birth if they allowed me to go over my dates. The doctor went away, and when he came back he told me that I was to come into hospital on Sunday 27th October, ready for me to be induced on the 28th, Monday. Michael made arrangements for some time off work, and on the Sunday, my in-laws came to look after Ginnette, whilst Michael took me to Solihull hospital, where I was taken up to ward M3 and settled in. I hated leaving Ginnette, I was her mum and no one could look after her like I could, and though deep down, I knew that no harm would come to her, it just seemed wrong for me to be away from her. She was only 19 months old, and wouldn't understand why I wasn't at home.

Once I was settled in, Michael had to go. I knew that I would see him the next day, but I couldn't tell him what time I would be going onto the labour ward to give birth. When a nurse came round to take my blood pressure and temperature, I asked if she knew what time I was going to be induced, but she said that she had no idea. With nothing to do but wait, I read a magazine that I had brought into the hospital with me. I knew It was going to be a long, long day, as Michael would not be able to visit me again today, because he had the task of looking after Ginnette.

Before too long, I was 'de-fluffed', and given the obligatory enema. The tube was so cold as it was inserted into my rear end, and by contrast the liquid felt warm as it gurgled its way up into my bowel. I had to lie still for five minutes, but it seemed more like thirty minutes to me, as my stomach lurched and rumbled, and I felt my butt cheeks squeeze ever tighter. I took a sharp intake of breath,

Lollipops, Bubblegum, Death and Lies

and the nurse told me, 'on your marks, get set....go!'. Good God, I did go...as fast as I could!, all the time hoping that the toilet was vacant. My butt remained nice and firm through all the clenching that I was doing, and luckily I made it to the loo in time. I had hoped that the enema would start me off, but no, not a twinge.

As I lay in bed trying to sleep, I thought of Michael and Ginnette and wondered if all was OK, and I also remembered the words of my Mum, when I told her I was pregnant the first time around, she said, 'It's the hardest days work you will ever do....hence the word **Labour**', but the best one of hers was, 'A woman is closer to death when she is giving birth, than at any other time in her life'. Mmmm... just the words I wanted to hear. I said a prayer and slowly drifted off to sleep.

I was woken the next morning at 7.30am, and I went for a bath, cleaned my teeth and combed my hair, then I went down to the 'day' room and had breakfast and a cup of tea. I chatted to the other women there, all awaiting the arrival of their babies, then went back into the ward to wait until I was sent for. At 11.30am, I was told that I was going down to the labour ward for my induction, but that because the previously epidural I'd been given when I was expecting Ginnette didn't work, there was no point giving me one this time. Once in the labour ward, I had a monitor strapped round my waist, which omitted a 'beep' as a continuous piece of paper escaped from the machine that I was connected to. This monitor apparently showed the baby's heart beat and whether or not it was in distress. I was then given an injection in the back of my hand, so all I had to do now was lie on my back and wait, while nurses came in and out, occasionally checking the machine to make sure all was going well.

Once my tummy started to go hard, I knew that my labour had started, and I felt optimistic for this baby. I was a little more sure, a little more calm this time. A midwife came and checked the machine, then listened to my tummy with the 'trumpet' and assured me that everything was fine. Although there were no scans back then, I knew in myself that this baby would be bigger than my previous two had been. By 1.00pm the contractions were very regular, and although I didn't feel ready to push, I knew that it wouldn't be that long before our family would increase in number by one. I was hot, and I was in pain, but I refused the gas and air offered to me as

Lollipops, Bubblegum, Death and Lies

I had read that it can make the baby drowsy, and believe me, I wanted this baby to help me and not be sluggish on it's journey,...If I had to work, so did 'it'!!.

The hospital staff had phoned to get a message to Michael, but, through no fault of his own, he hadn't arrived, so at 1.10pm, that was it, I wanted to push, and as the midwife performed the episiotomy, I could hear again Michaels complimentary words to me, after I had given birth to Ginnette,...'Tough as an old leather bucket'!. Bloody Hell!, my heart was racing so fast, my tummy went hard then soft again, and I welcomed the chance to rest for a minute or two. As I pushed once again, I could hear the rustle of the plastic pinafore that the midwife was wearing, and the murmur of the nurses talking. Then by 1.50pm I had done it, I had given birth to a blonde haired little boy who weighed in at 7lbs 14ozs. Michael and I had already decided to name the baby Victoria if it was a girl, and Karl Andrew if it was a boy, so Karl Andrew it was. He was beautiful, he had strong looks and could never be mistaken for a girl. He really was gorgeous!.

Michael had walked into the room just as it was all over, and Karl was lying in his 'see through' cot at the foot of the bed. He came over to me and gave me a kiss, and I told him that he now had a son. I could hear Karl sucking away at his fist, and Michael went over to have a look at his new son, of whom he said, 'He'll do'...!!. He then gave Karl a cuddle, told me he would see me that evening, then gave me a kiss and left to go back to work again.

I was kept in the labour room waiting for a doctor to come and stitch me up, and once again I was trussed up like a turkey as the midwife placed my ankles in the stirrups ready for the doctor to do his duty. I can still recall lying on my back, just about able to see the 'crown' of the doctors head as he delved into my nether regions, then a hand would come up between my legs and down again, as he merrily stitched away. He pushed on my still swollen tummy and said, 'you're bleeding from somewhere, but I don't know where', then spoke to the midwife and left. I didn't ask what he meant, and no one thought to tell me, but My legs were lowered again and I was left to rest. A little while later a nurse came in and washed me, then gave me a much welcomed cup of tea, after which I was taken up to the ward with Karl in tow. I was put to bed, and as I lay on my side and looked at my little baby lying contentedly in

Lollipops, Bubblegum, Death and Lies

his cot, I decided that I was not going to put myself through the same worries that I had when I had given birth to Ginnette. I was not even going to <u>attempt</u> to breast feed this baby, so when at feed time a three ounce bottle was brought for Karl, I immediately took it, and he devoured all of it.

Later that evening after visiting, when Michael had gone home, I went for a bath. I put a good cup full of salt into the bath, and I lowered myself into the refreshing water. I felt so clean, but when I got out of the bath to dry myself ,blood dripped onto the floor, so I quickly put on a 'pad', and went back to the ward. Once Karl had been taken to the nursery after his 10.00pm feed, I settled down for the night, and hoped that I would get some much needed sleep.

Karl was feeding well and putting weight on, so after the fifth day he was actually discharged, but this time <u>I</u> wasn't, as my bleeding still wasn't slowing down. I knew that the doctor was due to do his rounds, and I wanted desperately to go home, after all Ginnette would soon forget me if I stayed any longer. So I had a plan, that if I used the bidet before the doctor came round, he would let me go home, as it would look like the bleeding was slowing down. The doctor came round with the nurse, and the curtain was drawn round me. He looked at the notes, then at my tummy, and then he asked me a few questions, but when he pressed on my delicate tummy, the bleeding started again.

He said something then that made me want to curl up and die, 'it's a bit smelly down there, and I'm not too sure that something isn't right, so I'm not prepared to let you go home yet'. I wanted to shake him and shout at him, 'then tell me what's wrong, you're the doctor, not me!', but I had to accept that his decision not to allow me home was final. I couldn't understand why, because I was having a salt bath every day and doing everything right. When I got back in bed, once again I cried, I cried for Michael, I cried for Ginnette, and I cried because I wanted to go home

A nurse came in and sat on my bed, and she asked me what was wrong, so I told her that I was going to 'sign' myself out, that I'd had enough, and no one was doing anything about the bleeding. I was missing Ginnette and Michael, and I wanted to be in my own home. She then explained to me that if I signed myself out, there was a great possibility that if I did haemorrhage, a doctor might not come out to me, and that this hospital might refuse me re-admission. She Then told me that a doctor would be round later to talk to me about it.

After feeding Karl and settling him down, I had my lunch, but afterwards, when I went to use the bidet, I knew straight away that something was very wrong. The water in the bidet had turned bright red, and huge clots of blood were coming away from me, so I rang the 'panic' button, and a nurse opened the door and saw it for herself. I was shaking badly, so she and another nurse helped me into bed and told me to lie still. When the doctor came back to see me again, he examined me, then told me that I would have to go to the operating room, as he thought that some of the placenta had been left behind after giving birth. I was given an injection, but, because I'd had a cup of tea only minutes before using the bidet, I had got to wait until 8.00pm before I could go and have this procedure, which was sometimes called a D & C, or a 'scrape'.

When Michael left again after visiting hours had finished, I took my glasses off and took out my false teeth, (I only needed a wooden leg to complete the 'hat trick'!), but I refused to speak because I wasn't going to show off my empty gums for anybody. Once I was in the operating room, I was given another injection.

Now, I don't know if it was whilst I was under the anaesthetic, or when I was 'coming round', but I had a vivid dream that I had died, and I could hear people saying, 'that's it she's gone'. I then heard an echo of my name, and when I opened my eyes, I could see a 'halo' of light behind a figure. I must have then drifted in and out of consciousness, because the next thing I remembered was thinking to myself, 'Christ, I'm dead, I can feel myself going up!'. It was all so surreal, but I subsequently found out that I was actually going up,...In the lift!.

The next day, I still felt as though I was in a dream, that I was dead, and I was looking down on myself, it was all very peculiar, very, very peculiar!. However, my reward for this traumatic experience came in the form of my glasses and my false teeth, so I could now see, and I could smile at people!!.

Later that day, a nurse came and took my temperature and blood pressure. She told me that my temperature was on the high side, and forewarned me that possibly, when the doctor came and looked at my notes, he may say that until my temperature had come down, I would not be able to go home. She also told me that there had been some placenta left behind after giving birth, and that this had been the cause of my haemorrhaging. I was pleased that they had found the cause of my bleeding, and I was pleased that I would now be returning to my normal 'bodily functions'. My temperature might be high, but I felt sure it would go down once I was in my own home.

After a further four hours, the nurse came round again to take my blood pressure and temperature, and she left the thermometer in my mouth as she went over to another patient. Before she returned, I quickly took it out of my mouth, and dunked it into my cold glass of squash, hoping that it would appear to show that my temperature had come down, then I popped it back into my mouth just as the doctor appeared. He came over to my bed and asked how I was feeling, so I nodded my head, then he removed the thermometer and looked at it, 'A bit on the low side', is all he said!!. He examined me, spoke to the nurse, then he told me that I could go home, but once there I must rest as much as possible,..... OK, OK, OK!!. Yes !, I was going home. When Michael came to visit me the same evening, I asked him to bring my clothes in the next day, as I was free, at last.

Chapter 24

NEW HOME, NEW LIFE.

When Michael brought Karl and me home, I went through the front door first, and I heard Mums voice from the living room asking Ginnette if she knew who this was, then I stuck my head around the door. Ginnette was wary at first when I bent down to give her a kiss, but then I cuddled her, and I told her that Daddy would be up in a minute with her new baby brother. When Michael entered the living room holding Karl, I took Ginnette over to him and told her that this was her new brother who was going to stay with us. I don't think for a minute that she fully understood that he was here for ever!!. She showed no signs of jealousy, she didn't slap him, she didn't pinch him or pull his hair, but she still needed me, she still wanted my attention, and why shouldn't she, she was only 19 months old herself.

Lollipops, Bubblegum, Death and Lies

Life went on as normal, and every Friday morning at 7.30am, after Michael had left for work, I would put the made up feed bottles, nappies and nappy liners into the pram tray, then take the pram down the outside stairs. I would then take both children down, and laying Karl in the pram and sitting Ginnette in the back, facing Karl, I would walk the three miles or so to Chelmsley Wood where my Mum lived. Once we were there, Ginnette would have some breakfast, Karl would have a bottle, then I would then leave Ginnette with Mum whilst I took Karl with me to do Mum's shopping. Mum would give me 50p to buy a little toy for Ginnette, and although Mum was diabetic, I was always told to buy a couple of cream cakes, so that Mum and I could have them with a cup of coffee made with evaporated milk. When I got back, whilst Ginnette and Karl had their afternoon sleep, Mum would get out the playing cards and we would have a game of rummy or suits. On the occasions that I won, Mum would laugh and call me a cheating sod, I would give her some playful back chat, and the tears of laughter would stream down our faces as the banter continued. It was all so simple, but now after all the years that have passed by, so meaningful. I would usually give Ginnette her tea at Mums, then Michael would come and pick us up after he had finished work and take us home.

Mum was still in a relationship with Maurice. but I was never very keen on him, and I felt it was sometimes more of a mother/son relationship with them, as Mum would do his washing, ironing, and cooking, and look after him as she had done with her own offspring, but I have come to realise that she was quite happy with this arrangement. The one thing that I could never bring myself to accept was the sleeping arrangements,.. one bedroom with one double bed. To me he was only ever a 'part time' lover, as he would only spend Friday, Saturday, Sunday and Wednesday with Mum, and he would then spend the rest of the week back in his own house, with his father, his sister, and her young son.

Once home I would bath Ginnette and clean her teeth, then a short story and off to bed for her, then Karl would have his bath, a feed, and be put into his cot. Once the kids were settled, I would see to dinner for Michael and myself. As Money was always tight, many times we would have 'mushy pea boats' as a cheap meal. I would open a tin of spam, cut it in half, pipe some instant mash around the edges, then scoop mushy peas on top. All I had to do then was pop it into the oven to cook. By the time our tea was ready it, would often be approaching 8.30pm, and once we had finished our meal, I would wash up, then make up Karl's bottles. Karl would have his feed, have his nappy changed, and be settled down to sleep again, and luckily, unlike Ginnette, he was a good eater, and always slept well. My Last tasks would be to change the sterilizer and then put fresh 'Nappisan' in the bucket, ready for the next day. A very ordinary life continued like that for us, and we really were a contented family.

Our holidays were usually by courtesy of Michael's Mum and Dad. We loved going to the chalet at Dunster beach, and we loved the freedom and the walks, especially along the golf course. When the tide had gone out, little pools of water were left behind, and Ginnette would love to paddle in these, enthusing over the seashells, and collecting the pebbles and shells in her little bucket. She would get so excited when she found a half dead crab, and showed no fear of picking it up. After our evening walk, once back inside the chalet, we would all have a hot drink, then I would get Ginnette to stand up in the sink so that I could wash her down before going to bed, with the bowl being big enough to act as a bath for Karl. With both the children settled down to sleep, we would draw the curtains, I would make us a cup of tea, and Michael and I would watch the television or read a magazine before settling ourselves down to the sound of the soft rustling from the trees just outside our chalet.

The next morning we would wake to the sound of the ducks calling for their breakfast of dried bread. I was usually first up, so I would give Michael his cup of tea, dress Ginnette and Karl, then as they went with Michael to feed the ducks, I would prepare our breakfast. The whole site was awash every morning with the mouth watering aroma of bacon cooking, as it was almost part of the ritual and tradition of being at Dunster Beach!.

Too soon our holidays were over, and the time came for us to leave Dunster and travel back to Sheldon. I would feel so upset, as I never wanted to go back home. To me Dunster seemed a natural place to be, but we had to go, and I would dream of one day of owning our own property down that way, not just for a holiday period, but to live and retire there. Back at home the old familiar routines resumed, and Michael would go off to work, while I remained a full time mother and housewife.

Lollipops, Bubblegum, Death and Lies

Ginnette and Karl were growing up fast, and just like a birds nest when the fledglings grow, our flat was becoming a noticeably smaller, and sometimes unsafe place to bring two small children up in. Firstly, the concrete stairs at the side of our flat posed a problem, because Ginnette's natural instinct was to explore. I always worried that she would somehow escape the safe confines of our home, fall down the stairs and hurt herself. Secondly, when I needed to hang out the washing, I would have to wait until Karl was asleep and Ginnette was occupied with some childish activity. I would then creep to the door, lock it, and rush to the communal garden to hang out the washing before Ginnette noticed that I was not in the flat with her. One day, I was in the process of hanging out the washing , when I panicked as I heard a little voice calling 'Mummy!'. When I looked up, Ginnette was leaning out of the window calling to me. I shouted up to her to close the window, and that I would be up in a minute, and leaving the washing where it was, I rushed up to her. She had somehow pulled a chair across the living room floor, climbed up on it, and had opened the window!. I only retrieved the washing later that evening once

Michael had got home from work, as naturally it had become the least of my priorities!.

Michael and I agreed that it was time to move to a bigger house. We both knew that owning our own property was out of the question since Michael was in a low income bracket. In fact, when he went to see if we could get a mortgage, he was told that we could be only be given a mortgage if we could find a property for about £3,000. We might have been able to buy an old, run down, and in need of much renovation type of house, but we needed somewhere that was ready to move into. We decided to contact Birmingham City Council, who told us that we could be placed on the Redditch overspill housing register, and as Ginnette was nowhere near to starting school, we both felt that a move to Redditch would not pose a problem for us.

After a few weeks of hearing nothing from the council, Michael phoned them up, and they told him that there was no property available in Redditch after all, but there was some in Tamworth, Staffordshire, (the 'back of beyond' according to my Mum). To be honest, I didn't care where it was as long as we were out of the flat. I just couldn't afford to take the chance that Ginnette or Karl might end

Lollipops, Bubblegum, Death and Lies

up falling out of the window just because I needed to get the washing hung out.

So the waiting game to hear from Tamworth Council started, and In the meantime, Ginnette and Karl's 'playground' remained on the veranda. On the sunny days, I would fill up Ginnette's old baby bath with water, and she would love to sit in it and splash. So one beautiful day, I filled the bath up for her, but as she went to step in, her hand caught the side of the bath, and I watched in slow motion as I couldn't stop the bath from tipping over, and the water cascading over the edge of the veranda!. I immediately heard a shrill scream from below, and as I looked over the balcony, there was our downstairs neighbour, soaked from head to foot, her hair plastered to her head, and a sodden newspaper lying on the floor next to her!. I sheepishly shouted down with my apologies, and luckily, she saw the funny side of it and told me not to worry. I decided that perhaps the bathroom would be a far safer place for all concerned next time!!.

Ginnette and Karl would love it when I took them to Sheldon park, as there under my watchful eye, they could have a little run around, and I would push them on the swings. They would both tire themselves out, but it was Karl who would always fall asleep on the way back home.

Ginnette had also started going to a little local 'playgroup'. She would usually play there on her own, but would often come out afterwards holding out a painting she had done for me. I loved them and always felt really proud of them, so much so that I still have them today, with paint so thick that it cracks when I open them now.

We eventually received a letter from Tamworth Council asking us to go for an interview, so Mum came over to baby-sit Ginnette and Karl whilst Michael and I went over to Tamworth. Once there, we were called into an office and asked a series of questions, such as why did we want to move to Tamworth, and did we know anything of the history of Tamworth?. We were told that the only way we could get back to Birmingham once we'd completed the move, would be to get a private house exchange. After an hour or so of interviews and documentation, he handed to us a set of keys and gave us an address where we could go and look at a three bedroom house on Glascote Heath.

It took us some time to find it, but we eventually found 47,Maitland, though I thought it strange that there were no street,

Lollipops, Bubblegum, Death and Lies

road, or even avenue suffixes in this area. The house was set in a 'service road', not like the main road our flat was on in Sheldon, and I thought how peculiar the 'layout' of the estate seemed. We parked our car in a cul-de-sac, then had to walk along the path and under a 'bridge' flat, that was attached to the house we had come to view. Michael put the key in the lock and opened the front door, and were immediately impressed with how big it was compared to our flat in Church road. We had fun exploring that house for the first time, as there was an extra downstairs toilet for a start, a kitchen and dining room, a separate living room, and upstairs three big bedrooms, and a combined bathroom and toilet. A back door in the kitchen/dining room led out to the garden, which had a six foot wall around it, with a tall lockable back gate, and I knew that here, both Ginnette and Karl would be able to play in their own garden safely, for the first time in their young lives. I would be able to hang out the washing, without worrying that at any minute, a little hand would open the window and call out 'Mummy!'.

After we had finished looking over the house, we locked it up, and Michael and I talked about the effects of leaving Birmingham and moving to Tamworth. We decided that there was too much to lose if we didn't accept it, so before we left, Michael drove around the estate and some of the surrounding areas, to make sure we were generally happy with the outlook. When we then returned to the Tamworth Council offices, we told them that we would like to accept the property, and he informed us that we would be hearing from them in due course. When we got back to Sheldon, Mum asked us how it went, so while we were having our dinner, we told her of all that had transpired that day.

The next week seemed to drag by, and I felt sure that the move was going to be called off, that we would have a letter telling us that there was a more needy family, and that the house had gone to them instead of us. I was loath to 'count my chickens before they had hatched', so I didn't do any packing as I didn't want the disappointment of having to unpack everything again. Then one day, after Michael had gone to work, a letter was posted through our door bearing the Tamworth post mark, which I hoped was good news. When I opened the letter, I could hardly wait for Michael to come home as it was good news, telling us that we could pick up the keys for 47,Maitland, Glascote Heath, Tamworth.

So In May 1976, we started to pack our

belongings, and bit by bit we transported the more manageable items over to our new house. On the actual day of the 'full' move, my in-laws came and helped us, and the first thing we did was to make sure that the beds were made up, and ready for sleeping in, just in case the little people had had enough. But, no they hadn't, because their new found happiness was the garden, which soon became full of their toys. The staircase also became an new adventure to them, as the flat we had just left behind obviously didn't have stairs for them to climb, other than the concrete steps outside the flat which they were not allowed to play on anyway. We couldn't have been more fortunate, as that year,1976, from May till early October, was one of the warmest on record, and a hose pipe ban soon came into force. After Ginnette and Karl had finished playing in the paddling pool for a day, we would re-use the water out of it to water the few roses and other flowers that were growing in the garden. Occasionally my next door neighbour and her three children would come round for the afternoon, and while we drank tea and chatted, the children would play, argue, fight, then play again, and still moan when it was time for them to go home.

Michael and I felt fortunate to have this new home, but we'd had our furniture for some years and it was becoming the worst for wear. When we decided to replace it, we went to a furniture shop in Tamworth and ordered a new, brown striped, 'G-plan' suite. On the way home, I began to wonder if we had done the right thing, as it was a lot of money to us, at £8.32p per month, and we were now committed to pay that for the next three years!.

I had managed to get both Karl and Ginnette into the small playgroup opposite our local shops, so the paintings that they both did started to pile up. Karl was far more outgoing than Ginnette, and he preferred to play with the cars and building blocks, whereas Ginnette was a little more inhibited. Often she would just be sitting there sucking her thumb when I went in to collect them, and It worried me that she was not interacting as well as she should.

Michael was always the 'arty' one, so in 1977, when the playgroup held a fancy hat parade to commemorate Queen Elizabeth II's 25 years on the throne, it was he who made the hats for Ginnette and Karl. He made Ginnette an early Elizabethan hat with beads and jewels round it, and Karl had a 'quality street' regency type soldier's hat. When they came out from playgroup, every child had been given a silver jubilee commemorative coin, and our two still have theirs even now!.

When Ginnette was five years old she started at Lakeside Primary school, and though I'm not saying that she loved school, I had no trouble actually getting her there. I would go and bring her home for her lunch then take her back to school again, and I always collected her when school was over. She was progressing well, or so I thought, then one parent's evening we were told that Ginnette quite often 'switched off' in class. I asked her teacher if she thought that Ginnette needed remedial classes, but I was met with, 'Oh no, we have far worse children than Ginnette here!', so I left it at that.

That Christmas of 1978, Ginnette had a Sindy doll with a caravan, and Karl had a 'state of the art' Action man with moving eyes, which was complimented by a 'macho' jeep. Ginnette and Karl played together for hours behind the settee with these toys. Ginnette would tell Karl, "pretend Action man has come to see Sindy for some pop and crisps", and Action man would then be sat at the table along with Sindy, and then you'd hear Ginnette, in her 'American' accent, ask Action man, "do you want another drink?". This role play would last quite happily until Christmas lunch was ready. When we had finished our Christmas lunch, the children would resume their play, and Michael and I would 'crash out' in front of the television, not to listen to the Queens speech, but to watch some long awaited film to be shown. Erm... film, or Queen... Queen, or film?, there was no contest really, especially as I am not particularly patriotic, and anyway isn't it a treasonable offence to crack open your nuts whilst the queen is talking, and you're 'deafing' her out'?!.

The following morning when I got up, I was feeling ill and quite nauseous, but considered that It must be due to something I had eaten. I still felt off colour for the next few days, and then it happened, I missed my period. I was twenty eight years of age, and life was beginning to feel really satisfying, so the last thing I wanted now was to be pregnant again. I took a water sample to the doctor's surgery, and on New Years eve I phoned them to get the results, and yes, I was definitely pregnant. Somehow I managed to say, 'Oh how lovely', when what I really wanted to shout was, 'Oh no!, Bugger me backwards with a barge pole, I can't be!'.

Chapter 25

A NEW LIFE STARTS, AND ANOTHER LIFE ENDS.

Just because we'd moved to Tamworth didn't mean that I had stopped going over to Chelmsley Wood to see my Mum. One Friday, when I told Mum that I was pregnant again, she offered this kindly advice,.....'Tell him to tie a knot in it'!, and that was it, no congratulations, no throwing of arms round me, nothing at all.

During that pregnancy, I first had a threatened miscarriage, and spent eight days in the hospital at Burton-on-Trent, then at sometime during the first trimester I caught German measles. A blood test confirmed that I had never had German measles at any time in my life, so therefore there was a chance that my unborn child could be damaged. I was five months pregnant by the time I had received the full results, so it was too late for me to do anything about it, even if I had decided to have an abortion, a procedure, which to be honest ,I had never agreed with anyway. Not long afterwards, just to 'cap' it all, I fell down a flight of concrete stairs in our local Co-op store!. The staff there advised me that I should go to see a doctor, just to make sure that everything was fine with the baby, but when the doctor examined me, he told me that I was far more shaken up than the baby, so I decided there and then that this baby must be a fighter.

As far as the remainder of the pregnancy went, I sailed through it, and the problems only came when I had reached my due date of 9th August. The Gynecologist at the clinic was extremely nonchalant, almost to the point of being insulting about my concerns, and told me to go home, and stop worrying about my going into labour. Despite my trying to explain to him that I had already had a problematic still birth, and that I had been induced with both the previous pregnancies, he still maintained that I would go into labour 'naturally'.

I went out in tears, and when I told Michael, who'd been waiting for me with Ginnette and Karl in the car outside, I remember saying that if anything happened to this unborn child

Lollipops, Bubblegum, Death and Lies

because of <u>this</u> 'so called expert' opinion, I would swing for him. I just wanted to get home, but Michael got out of the car, and went back into the receptionist, and asked to see the doctor who had just seen me. I hated making a fuss, but Michael had gone before I could object. On his return he said to me, "Right, you're going into Burton hospital tomorrow!". When I asked Michael what he had said to the doctor, he told me that he first of all he'd asked this Doctor if he had even looked at my records, but that he very much doubted it!. He then told him, that if he had bothered himself to do so at all, he would have recognised that I was more than entitled to have my concerns about giving birth naturally. Michael then said that despite the recorded problems with my previous pregnancies, and the various problems with this one, no psychology whatsoever had been applied to the case, and that he'd already lost one daughter through a hospital 'blunder' of this nature. After telling the Doctor that he seemed to be running his clinic like a cattle market, Michael then told him that he would, on record, hold HIM personally responsible if I had another still birth!.

That was one up to Michael, but now I worried that I was going to be seen as a troublemaker and therefore perhaps would be shunned at the hospital.

The next day, when I got to Burton Hospital, I was shown to the ward, and would you believe it?,....that night I went into false labour!. However, the following morning I was still no nearer to having the baby, and so I wanted to know the reason why I was not being induced if I had already had contractions. I was told that the doctor would be round later that morning, and that I could ask him directly. Imagine my horror when it was the same doctor that I had seen the day before in the clinic, the very same one Michael had 'spoken' to. So, in for a penny-in for a pound, I decided to ask him, but I only got as far as, "Could I ask you a question please?", and he just curtly replied, "I should think your husband has all the answers, Mrs Brown", and walked away. He might just as well have slapped me in the face, and the staff were just as shocked as I was by the looks on their faces. It was FIVE days later when I was finally taken down to the labour ward, where at 11.50am, I <u>did</u> have to be induced yet again, and then at 1.10pm, on 15th August 1979, Stephen was born. He weighed 8.0 lbs, looked like a miniature version of Winston Churchill, and I loved him, instantly!.

Lollipops, Bubblegum, Death and Lies

Back home again, life for us carried on very much the same as it had always done, though with one more mouth to feed. I still managed to get over to see Mum, along with the three children, and in between Stephen sleeping, and Ginnette and Karl drawing (or playing with my Mum's clean bandages, which were meant for her ulcerated leg!), I would clean her flat, make her a cup of coffee, and wash up etc.. Maurice was still her 'part time' lover, and I still felt the same dislike towards him being there as I had done for many years. One Friday when we visited Mum, she was quite poorly, off her food and drink, and she was being sick. I phoned for the doctor, who, when he came out, said that Mum in his opinion, had either got gall stones, or that the pancreas was not making enough insulin, so he prescribed extra Metformin tablets for her, and with that he left.

The following week, Mum looked really terrible, although as usual she maintained that she was alright. When I went home, I phoned Elwyne and told her of my concerns, so she said that she would go and look in on Mum. When Elwyne rang me back later, she told me that Mum had said the same thing to her, that she was fine.

So my visits to Mum carried on, and one

day when Stephen was nine months old, I told Mum that if she could hold Stephen on her lap, I would take her out in her wheelchair for some fresh air. Ginnette, to this day remembers this occasion, because whilst Mum was holding Stephen, Karl climbed onto her lap as well, then Ginnette, not wanting to be left out also clambered onto Mums lap. My God, my Mum on her own was about 16 stone!, so imagine how much weight I was pushing with all four on the wheelchair. No wonder I was practically on my knees by the time I got back to her house!!.

Mum was taken into Heartlands hospital in May1980 as she was having a lot of pain by this time. When I phoned to see how she was, I was told that she had just gone down to the operating theatre to have the gall stones removed, and to phone back later that day. When I did ring back, I was asked if I could come into the Hospital as the doctor needed to talk to me. So the following day I went along and when I spoke to the doctor, I suppose that if I was half expecting bad news, that's exactly what I got.

Apparently, during the operation they had found cancer in Mum's liver, and that it was terminal. I asked them what they would tell Mum, as she would have expected

Lollipops, Bubblegum, Death and Lies

to be feeling a little better, having had the gallstones removed, but the doctor said that they had in fact left the gall stones 'in situ'. There was no 'key hole' surgery back then, and they hadn't wanted to put Mum through any more pain than necessary from a further, more extensive surgical operation. When I asked him if he could give me an approximate length of time that she had left to live, he couldn't, other than to say that Mum would have a slow climb to the top of a hill, metaphorically, but once she had reached that plateau, it would be a swift descent to her end. And how right he was!.

Mum came home from hospital, and for the next three months she carried on as if things were getting back to normal. They say 'ignorance is bliss', and so none of Mum's offspring told her that she had cancer, though I do wonder to this day if I had done the right thing by not telling her. I clearly remember that it was on the 31st July 1980, thirteen years to the day after John had committed suicide, that Mum was rushed back into hospital, and on the 2nd August 1980, I received a phone call from Elwyne to say Mum had died. (This was Incidentally, just thirteen days before Stephens first birthday). The kids had been put to bed, and Michael was not there to comfort me as he was many miles away on a booking, but I asked Elwyne if she would meet me at the hospital as I wanted to say my last goodbye to Mum,...but what was I going to do with the kids?.

I decided to phone Michael's sister, Sally, and asked if her husband could take me to the hospital, and if his other sister, Susan could baby-sit for me. When they arrived, Susan kindly stayed and looked after the kids, whilst my brother in-law, John, took me all the way over from Tamworth to Heartlands Hospital in Birmingham, which was still quite a journey then. Once there, he went back home, and I waited in the corridor for Elwyne to arrive.

That is when I sobbed to myself, and things started going through my mind once again. Although I was relieved to think that Mum was at last out of her pain, in my head I was also thinking, 'you never knew, you never knew what John had done to me'. I felt a sense of pride in myself for never telling her, for making sure that I never had to see the hurt in her eyes from knowing that John, her favourite, had for whatever reason, taken advantage of me in the years that I was growing up.

When Elwyne arrived at the hospital , we made our way to the ward and told the Sister that we were here to see Mrs Fewtrell. She asked us to wait for a while as the nurses were just preparing Mum, but only five minutes later, the curtain around her was pushed aside, and Elwyne and I were led in to see her. I had never before seen a dead person, but lying there before Elwyne and myself was my Mum, her eyes closed, mouth slightly open, and her lips turned blue. I wanted to gently shake her to wake her up, and my tears streamed effortlessly down my cheeks and onto my top. I stroked Mum's head, just like she had done to comfort me when I was a small child, then I kissed her brow and told her to have a safe journey. Then I told her that I was glad that she was dead!, but it was not meant in any sense of 'Oh Goody, goody!', far from it, what I actually meant was, that I was glad she was now free of any pain.

Elwyne also stroked Mum's head, and kissed her, then she turned to me and told me that Mum was now with Dad and John. Good God!, I cried even more then, as the usual mixture of selfish thoughts ran through my head. With Elwyne's words ringing in my ears, I was afraid that although it would no longer affect me, Mum would find out about my misadventures with John. I knew that I could never, ever be sure that there is no after life, or that our beings are possibly reincarnated, so the chances of Mum meeting up with Dad or John were probably zero, and so my secret was still safe.

Before leaving the hospital, I was handed a hospital property bag, which contained Mum's wedding ring, her glasses, purse and hand bag, but on a lighter note, I'm glad that the hospital had disposed of her false teeth!, as God knows what I would have done with them, although I suppose I could have kept them for crimping the pastry!.

Michael, in the meanwhile had been home, where of course he was met by his sister who had told him the news about my Mum, and he eventually arrived at the hospital at about 12.45am. Elwyne and I had shed a few tears, and we had spoken of some of the funnier times with Mum, then we had shared a cigarette, the first one I'd had in over 10 years!. Michael and I had a hug , then, leaving Mum where she lay, we took Elwyne home. Before she got out of the car, Elwyne and I made a pact that neither of us would go to Mums house alone, but we would wait for each other, and because Elwyne worked full time, she left up to Michael and I to make the funeral arrangements.

On our way back to Tamworth from

Lollipops, Bubblegum, Death and Lies

Chelmsley Wood, I turned my head to the car passenger window and watched the road to my left with tears streaming down my face. As usual, I didn't want to make Michael aware that I was breaking my heart over the loss of my Mum. I was 30years old, married, with three beautiful children, and we had known hard times financially. I'd personally been through traumas, been blamed and shamed, but in spite of all that, it did not mean that I was tough enough to take Mums death in my stride. I felt unimaginable guilt at leaving her all alone in the hospital where the nurses or doctors might not treat her body with dignity. Oh my God, how was I going to tell Ginnette and Karl that their Nanny was dead?. Ginnette was only seven and a half, Karl was only just coming up to six years old, and Stephen wasn't yet a year old. They didn't understand life yet, how could I expect them to understand about death?.

While Michael took his sister back home to Belgrave, which was the next estate to ours, I made myself a cup of coffee, and almost scolded myself as my eyes magnified with tears. On his return, he kept apologising for not being at home when I'd got the phone call from Elwyne informing me of Mums death. But it wasn't his fault, as that night he'd had a booking, and was obligated by contract to go and play at the function. It's just a shame that we had no such a thing as a mobile phone that night, as it would have made it easier to contact him, but they were still in their infancy, and very, very, expensive.

Mum had died on the Saturday, but on the following day, Sunday, when Ginnette came down stairs, she already knew that Mum was gone. Don't ask me how, but she said that in the dark she'd looked out of her bedroom window and saw Nanny, who was surrounded by angels, and they were taking her up to heaven. My God, how could she have known?. Was it as some people claim, that certain children have some kind of sixth sense about these matters, or was it that she overheard my conversation with Elwyne the evening before, and her little mind was playing tricks on her?. What ever the reason may be, when I confirmed that Nanny was now in heaven, she just took it in her stride, better than I had. When I told Karl the news, there were no tears or questions, but Ginnette cried and asked Karl why he wasn't crying too. I wondered whether Ginnette had picked up on my own sadness, or if she really did realize that she would never see her nanny again?.

Lollipops, Bubblegum, Death and Lies

As for Karl, well, Lego bricks were far more interesting!.

On the Monday, 4th August, with the children again being looked after by Michael's sisters, Michael and I went to the Birmingham Co-Operative Funeral Directors offices to make the arrangements for Mums funeral, and it crossed my mind that if we'd have been given co-op dividends on funerals, we would have been rich by now, as that's where Mum had also arranged Dad and Johns funerals!!. The arrangements were duly made, and the Co-op would provide a French polished coffin, and a robe, make arrangements for the cremation, and provide one Hearse and two Limousines at a cost of £227.75. The fees at Perry Barr crematorium would be £36.00, Doctors fees were £27.50, and unfortunately for him the poor minister only received £9.00, so making a grand total cost of £300.25. Of course, we didn't receive any co-op dividends, but we were told that if we could make settlement within fourteen days, they would deduct £2.75. from the total...... Wow!!.

Even though the hospital knew that the cause of Mum's death had been cancer, they said that a post- mortem would still be needed to prove that it was indeed the cause of death. I hated the thought that some one was going to cut into Mums naked body, again believing that there would be no dignity shown, and inside I was angry. Hadn't she suffered enough, couldn't these people just leave her alone?, she was after all, dead, and had died in hospital. Unless there was a complete and utter 'nutcase' bumping the patients off, I felt there was no need to carry out the post-mortem. She had, after all died in their care, she'd already been cut open, I already knew that she had terminal cancer, so I couldn't get my head around the fact that a post-mortem needed to be carried out. Once again I never thought to seek advice for help in objecting.

Before the funeral took place, Elwyne and I would go to Mums once a week to start clearing out her belongings. We thought it only fair that Maurice should be given the chance to have some token of her, and we were quite happy to do so. Stan, on the other hand wanted nothing except old photographs of him and his wife and daughter. I can only say, in retrospect, that perhaps we were in too much shock and confusion and with mixed emotions, but some items of Mum's that were of special or sentimental value to Elwyne and myself, did suddenly go missing, and I have never seen them since. I can't point the finger of blame at anyone without proof, but given that Elwyne and I were always at Mum's house together, and knowing that Stan wanted nothing to do with any of the material things that belonged to Mum, it could only have been someone else who had a key to her house, someone who spent more than enough time there to know just where everything was kept.

Elwyne's marriage to Fred had broken down some years before. Due to Susan's death, like a lot of couples faced with the loss of a child, neither could compromise in their compassion for each other, and they had gradually grown apart. After a number of years alone, Elwyne had remarried, to a George Surridge, and they had set up home together on Chelmsley wood. George wasn't going to attend the funeral, but was staying home to put on a 'spread' ready for when we returned. I felt that Ginnette, Karl and Stephen were much too young to take to a funeral, after all they wouldn't understand the procedures and rituals that go with the death of anyone, so again calling on the help of Michael's sisters, I asked if they would look after all three of them, and It was quite a relief when they said they would do so.

On the day of the funeral, we arranged for everyone to meet at the Co-Op funeral parlour in Birmingham, as both Elwyne and I had agreed that because of the distances having to be travelled by some of the mourners, it would be a central point. It also provided for anyone wanting to say their last goodbye's to Mum of the chance to do so, as her coffin was lying in the chapel of rest and had not yet been closed. I had already said my last goodbyes to her in the hospital and I did not need to, nor did I want to see, my Mum, who rarely wore any make up in life, done up like someone who was going to jump out of the coffin for a night on the town. That would not have been <u>my</u> Mum, so I preferred to remember her as lying peacefully asleep on the hospital ward.

When the time came for us to take our places in the limousines, my throat was sore from holding back the tears, and we travelled in silence to Perry Barr Crematorium. As we turned into the gate, we saw people standing around the minister who was waiting outside for us, and when we got out of the limousine I watched as Mum's coffin was laid on the small wheeled trolley. No pallbearers shoulder high job for her!. That was the moment that did it for me. I thought that my legs would buckle

Lollipops, Bubblegum, Death and Lies

under me, and I wanted to jump on the coffin with her. She shouldn't make that journey alone, I wanted her to have company. I let my grief surface for once, my sobs becoming louder, and I whispered 'Mum'. I had never truly told Mum, or shown her, how much I loved her, and yet, I had to remind myself of the guilty secret I had never told her about.

Old memories of Dad's and John's funerals now came flooding back, and I wonder now, if those, combined with losing Mum, had exacerbated my emotions. My heart was pounding, my face had reddened, and I was feeling hot. My God I wanted her back, God?, God!. This only went to confirm that there was no God for me now. I felt that I had been deserted, and I hated God, yet here I was, in this church, to praise him and thank him in celebration of Mum's life. I couldn't hold back my heavy sobbing any longer, and both Michael and Elwyne linked their arms in mine. Melodramatic I know, but I really felt that it was not too late for me to jump onto the coffin and go with her!. Once again, hymns were sung and prayers were said, but then I became totally confused, because at the end of the service, Mum's coffin remained on the 'trolley' just in front of the conveyor belt. So when we all filed out of the church, and she still had not been lifted onto the belt, my mind told me that this wasn't final, as she was still lying there in the church!. All the way home, I felt that I had left something behind, even though I knew that Mums cremation would take place imminently.

Once back at Elwynes, I was too choked with emotion to have anything to eat, so Michael and I just had a cup of tea. I wanted to get back to my own home in Tamworth and to my children, my family, but then the small talk started about the times when my brothers and sisters were little, and how devious my mother could be.

There was a time, back in the 1940's, when Mum bought a loaf of bread, and after feeding the kids with half of it, she stuck a rusty nail in the other half and took it back to the shop. Mum then made a complaint to the Shopkeeper about it, and ended up coming back home again with a fresh loaf of bread!.

On another occasion, Stan and Elwyne were playing at cowboys and indians under the kitchen table, which they were pretending was a tent. But then they lit a campfire as they had seen the indians do at the cinema, except of course that this one set fire to the lino!. Needless to say, all hell broke loose

Lollipops, Bubblegum, Death and Lies

when Mum came into the room, and It's lucky that my brothers and sisters survived at all!

Something else that Elwyne did when she was about fourteen years old, was to light the wax candles on the Christmas tree, and like something out of a Tom and Jerry cartoon, a fire quickly took hold of the tree instead. Mum dashed in with a bucket of water and just threw it at the flames, but the tree was totally ruined, and didn't get replaced that year. I began to smile as I listened to these stories, and I felt sure that Elwyne must have harboured a secret passion to be an arsonist!.

Elwyne then retold a story that Mum had told me many times before, and it really explains the sort of person Mum could be when needs must. Apparently when my Dad was about sixteen, he had worked as a street gas lamplighter, and it seems that one evening, in the winter, he slipped with the pole in his hand. The pole had pierced the left side of his chest, and then had pierced the left ventricle of his heart. Although I don't know of any other details, it had left Dad with heart trouble for the rest of his life, and perhaps that was a factor in his early death. So the story goes, some years later Dad had been ill and off work for six weeks, and Mum,

Stan and Elwyne were getting by as best they could. However, only a few months before Dads illness, they had bought a new settee, to be paid off at a grand total of 5/- per week (25p in today's money). Because Dad was now off work, Mum had gone into the shop, and made an arrangement with the shop manager to make a reduction on the payments, and It was agreed that she would now pay just 2/- per week (10p).

Two days after Dad had returned to work there was a knock at the front door, and when Mum opened it, it was two bailiffs who had come to repossess the settee. Mum argued the toss with them, but they weren't listening, so Mum stepped aside and let them in, no doubt with a plan already formulating in her mind. As they entered the room where the settee was, Mum locked the front door, and proceeded to give Elwyne and Stan their dinner, but then as the bailiffs advanced to open the front door, they realized it was locked!. One man said, 'come on missus, let us out', but Mum told him that she would only open the door for them when her husband came home. They then started to shout at her, and Elwyne and Stan, being somewhat frightened went and hid behind Mums skirt. As she was going 'hammer and tongs' with the bailiffs, one of them tried to take the key from her hands, but she in turn held open the top of her blouse, dropped the key down there, and told them, "one step closer, and I'll shout RAPE!!". The bailiffs then backed down, and she did indeed make them wait until my Dad came home from work, without even giving them so much as a cup of tea!. As they listened to what Dad had to say, Mum said to them, " Now you've had the same information from him, so we could have saved all of this time and trouble, off you go now, tarrah". They left minus the settee, and no doubt, with their tails between their legs!!.

The stories that were told on that day of Mom's funeral put a smile back on my face, and although the traumas of my younger life still troubled me, I still felt lucky to be the youngest child of a large family.

Not long after Mum had died, Elwynes marriage to George had also broken down, and she went to live on the eighth floor of a tall block of flats on Chelmsley Wood. Although my visits to Mum had come to an end, I now started to visit Elwyne once every month, or six weeks or so, and I grew closer once again to the big sister that I had always looked up to.

With Mum no longer here, although I had

three small children to help take my mind off things during the daytime, I still had dreams about Mum that felt very realistic. Usually, It was almost as though she had been in the house to visit me, and to tell me that she was alright. However, one dream I had really 'freaked me out'. I was walking through a forest, the trees were full of leaves, and the sun was shining. I was talking to my Mum, and I told her that she should not be here now, as her rightful place was now up in heaven. Then she said to me, 'but I have come for you!'. So as I protested, 'I can't just leave the kids!', she mounted a bicycle and started to peddle away, and as she disappeared over the brow of a hill I could still hear her calling my name. Then just her hand appeared, being held out to me, and she told me to hold her hand and follow her, but the moment I went to reach for her hand, I woke with a start!. As much as I did love and still do love my Mum, I was not prepared to leave my children. It left me feeling very uneasy for the rest of that day, but I soon realised that there was no point in pondering over the meaning of a dream.

Chapter 26

OWNING OUR OWN PROPERTY

In 1982, three years after Mums had died, Michael looked again into the possibility of buying our own house. We knew that financially things would be very restricted, and that we would have to tighten our belts even more than we were already doing. My father-in-law helped us out by lending us the eight hundred pounds we needed for the deposit, so the task of house hunting began. It was such an exciting time for me, because at last, we would no longer be paying 'dead money' for a council house that would never be ours. Even though Margaret Thatcher, the first female prime minister was now encouraging people to buy their council houses from the local councils, and though I liked the house in Maitland, I certainly didn't want to buy it. We looked at quite a variety of houses before, somewhat naively, settling for one on Stonydelph, which was the next estate to Glascote Heath.

The cost of the house was £15,950.00, but It had no central heating, or double glazing, nor did it have a garage. It was, however a three bedroom, semi detached house, with its own drive for the Ford Cortina car that we now had. The house itself wasn't too bad, and the neighbourhood seemed better than the area we had moved from, and Ginnette and Karl were quick to make friends, both at school and with some of the new neighbour's children. Stephen was still too young to go to other neighbours houses to play, but he was content to play in the back garden with his toys, and sometimes the little girl who lived next door would come round to our house, where they played happily, and did not fall out too often.

We had only just settled into the new house when the recession started. Many people were quickly finding it hard to keep up with their mortgage, and we were no exception, but I would be damned if we had just got on the first rung of property ownership just to lose everything now, and then have to move off the 'ladder' again. If I had to starve myself to keep this house, then that is what

I was prepared to do,....except maybe when it came to Thornton's chocolates!.

A friend of mine told me that the Birmingham Evening mail was looking for agents in the Tamworth area to canvass on their behalf. It was three nights work for a basic wage of £10.00, and an extra 50p per new order that each individual agent got. Bloody hell, I realized that I would never make it into the big time when my maximum wage got to £13.00!, but it was better than nothing, and it was another £10 to £13 that could be put away for paying the bills.

One evening, as I was getting ready to go out canvassing, I'd had my wash and combed my hair, but when I went into our bed room, I sat on the bed and sobbed. I then heard Michael coming up the stairs, though not because he had heard me crying, he just happened to need to come upstairs for something. I quickly dried my eyes so that he would be none the wiser, but he noticed that my eyes were red, and asked me what was wrong. He said that we would get by, and not to worry about the mortgage. We weren't going to lose the house, as we had after all, been to see the building society manager and told him of our fears. They had been very helpful, and had managed to arrange it so that we were only paying off the interest, so that had made our repayments a little more manageable. However, my tears actually had nothing to do with any of that, and at that precise moment, I couldn't give a toss about the house. The tears started to silently fall again, and this time I found myself telling Michael my darkest secret, the secret that I had vowed, all those years back, that I would take to my grave with me. I have no idea why, at that precise moment, I felt that I needed to tell anyone, but I saw the look in Michael's eyes, and he really had no idea of what, if anything, to say to me. I knew that I couldn't stay at home and discuss it further, as I had my 'high profile' canvassing job to do, so Michael just hugged me tightly, then I put on my coat and left to do my job.

That evening, my mind was not on persuading the general public to buy the Evening Mail, instead I was cursing myself for letting out my secret. I felt so guilty, and I was so annoyed, and I felt that I had betrayed John. I did not want to discuss this further with Michael, or anyone else for that matter, and when I returned home, I had a cup of coffee and talked to Michael about the how the evenings work had gone. The subject of John and I had been pushed even further

Lollipops, Bubblegum, Death and Lies

back into some dark little corner of my mind, but Michael now knew. I saw no reason to go into any great detail, and Michael did not ever press me to talk about it.

The job didn't last for too many months, because our careers as high-flying agents for the Evening Mail never really got off to a good start. The people of Tamworth wanted their own local paper, the Tamworth Herald. That was it then, I could no longer contribute to the household bills, and without that extra money coming in we just about scraped by, but I can hold my head up and say 'we did it!'.

My roll of full time mother and housewife carried on, and by 1984, Ginnette was at high school, Karl was still in Junior school, and Stephen had started at primary school in the September. I found out quite by chance that one of the teachers at Stephens school was looking for someone to clean her house one day a week, and when I approached her, she was happy to accept me as her 'char'. So once a week, I cleaned her house for her, and for three hours work I earned £6.00. I thought things were going really well, when my next door neighbour, who worked all hours God sends, also asked if I would clean his house and do a bit of ironing for him every so often. I was now a full time 'Mrs Mop', and I did this work for both people until my neighbour bought himself another house, and left the area. That was one job down, but one remaining, and though it was bringing in a pittance, it was better than no job at all.

In 1986, I decided to put my name down as a supply 'dinner lady' at Stephen's school, as I knew that by doing this work, it would tie in with the children's school holidays. I thoroughly enjoyed those times there, and soon my supply job turned into a full-time dinner lady position. After some time there, I felt a certain amount of pride when the head teacher approached me and asked if I would be interested in working an extra 15 hours a week with a 'special needs' child. When I told her that I was not formally qualified to work with children, She also paid me a lovely compliment, by telling me that as far as she was concerned, I was more than qualified!. I had already been police CRB checked, so I was ready for the challenge, and my job as dinner lady continued along with my duties towards my special needs child..

He was a very clever, but vacant young lad, who was being tested for autism, and I eventually stayed and helped him for two years. The rewards of watching his progress

Lollipops, Bubblegum, Death and Lies

were incredible, and we built up a trusting, caring relationship. I took my responsibilities very seriously, though I always knew that if I was away from work for any reason, it would completely 'throw' him.

It was during 1986, that one day, after I had finished work, I was just preparing the tea, and had made myself a cup of coffee, when there was a knock at the door. When I answered it, there stood a work colleague of Michael's, who told me that Michael was in Good Hope hospital. He'd had an accident at work, falling down a flight of stairs, and they were concerned that he might have broken his back. Luckily, he hadn't, but he had ruptured two 'discs', damaged some of the nerves down his spine, and had torn some muscles in his back and pelvis, with the expected severe bruising. When he eventually returned to work after more than a month off, he found that none of his work had been kept up to date by anyone else in the office, and that he was expected to catch up with it as soon as possible, whilst at the same time dealing with any new work that came in.

Michael began to find it difficult to manage, and constantly worried that he could not do his best. Soon he started to lose weight, he would bleed from his rectum, and he was in a lot of pain. Reluctantly, he eventually went to the doctors, and after some minor tests he was informed that the Ulcerative colitis he had suffered with on and off since teenage, had flared up again. The doctor sent Michael to the hospital for a sigmoidoscopy and various other examinations and biopsies, and the results of these tests showed that Michael was now very ill with an inflamatory bowel problem. He was now losing a lot of time from work because of this illness, and because of the problems with lack of support at work, his mental health also started to deteriorate. Inevitably this meant that he had to lose even more time from work.

When he did return to work again, he had been transferred to another office, on work that he was not trained for, or felt confident about doing properly. He did his best, though constantly feeling under a lot of stress, but eventually it took its toll on his health again. So it was, in 1988, that Michael had a mental breakdown. After help from the right people in hospital, discussions with his employers, and much thought, he finished working for the foreseeable future. luckily by this time he had received a payment against the insurance claim which followed his accident, as well as a 'finishing' wage settlement from his employer, so we were able to manage, albeit with difficulty.

I had now been employed by Staffordshire County Council for two years when the head teacher approached me again to discuss the possibility of me 'going up' to the junior school with 'my boy'. She also suggested to me, that another option, for my personal benefit, would be to consider going to College full time, in order to gain my National Nursery Examination Board diploma. That night when I went home and considered those options, my mind was racing. I did not think that I was academically suited for college, but at the same time, I knew that if I didn't do something to turn my life around, and to look to the possibility of having to become the future 'bread winner', it was almost a certainty that our house could be repossessed. When I considered that 'My boy' would only have three years to complete at junior school, then where would that leave me?.

Michael did not really like the idea of me going to college, especially full time, but he agreed that I should at least 'put the feelers out', so the following day I told the Head teacher that I would not go on to junior school with 'my boy' after all. That decision would give Staffordshire Education Department plenty of time to employ someone else once he had moved up. I then told her that I was going to do my best to make sure I secured a college place for the N.N.E.B. course, starting that September, 1989.

Michael has always been excellent at letter writing, so that weekend he helped me to put a letter together requesting information on the N.N.E.B. course. Good Lord!, if I needed Michael to help me draft a simple letter, how on earth was I going to cope if I was accepted by the college?.

Just before the termination of my employment with the school, I received a letter from the college asking me to go and sit an entrance exam. Oh my God!, how on earth was I going to deal with that!. I had, after all, left school twenty four years earlier with no qualifications, and though I might well be older and maybe a little bit wiser, I was certainly no brighter academically. It would have been quite easy to phone the college and tell them some lie, that I had made a mistake, that I was leaving the country, or that I was pregnant with triplets!, but no, I had come this far and I needed to prove to myself that I would be at least in control of my future, which was to eventually and hopefully benefit us all.

In the July of 1989, I went along to the college and spoke to the course tutor, who informed me that if I was successful in obtaining a place, the course would be for a period of two years, and consisted of 60% college time, and 40% as placement time. My hours at college would be from 9.00am to 4.30pm. Then she handed a test paper to me, and told me that I had one hour to choose a subject and write about it. One of the questions was based around state education and private education,...well, that one was out for a start. The next question was on the development of a child between the ages of birth to six months, and the last one was regarding lines taken from a book, that the person sitting the exam had to find either a beginning, or an ending to, in their own words. I chose the latter, and after an hour I presented my paper (feeling as though it had been a complete failure) to the tutor. She told me that I would hear from the college in due course, then wished me in the meantime, 'good luck'.

When I came home from college I told Michael that I didn't hold out much hope, but that if push came to shove, I supposed I could always do my dinner lady's job again. Then during August I received a letter from

Tamworth college, and I thought this is it,.....a rejection. Secretly, in the bathroom, and already geared up for disappointment, I tentatively opened the envelope. Good God!, I <u>had</u> passed and was accepted on the course!. I was to enrol for the N.N.E.B. course in the first week of September 1989. It was only then I realized that I had a lot of work, time and effort to look forward to, but little did I know then how hard it would be for me.

I told Michael, quite nonchalantly, that I had been accepted. but he wasn't really happy about it, mainly because he thought that he had let me down, and that I was being forced to do something because of our financial circumstances. It also meant, that with his health at such a low ebb, he would miss me during the day. Later, we talked some more about it, and I think it eventually sunk in that this was the only way forward for us. It wasn't as though the kids were little anymore, though I knew that they still needed their Mum. Ginnette had just left school and was working at a local chemist, Karl was doing well at senior school, and Stephen was to start senior school in the September, so I wasn't too concerned. After all their Dad would be there for them when they returned home, in Ginnette's case, from work, and from school in Karl and Stephen's case.

Chapter 27

BACK TO SCHOOL!

September soon arrived and I got myself off to college, where we got to know which group we were to be in, and got to know each other. I was glad to say, that I was not the only 'wrinkly', (an affectionate term for a mature student!) there. Out of twenty one new students starting the course, there were four mature students, including myself, and the younger students, although they were probably 'pains in the arses' of their own parents, were absolutely brilliant towards us older ones.

I soon settled into essays and assignments, as well as a home routine, but the going was tough. In December I was given the project of making a hanging mobile, along with three essays, and three child observations to write up!. It was then I wondered, 'what the bloody hell have I taken on?'. Christ, another two years of this lay ahead!. The work load was enormous. It was bad enough for a teenage girl to cope with, but for me it was twice the work, as I also had a family to look after, as well as a husband who was suffering bad health. Some evenings I would do my 'homework' and crawl into bed at 1.30am next morning. With Christmas looming, I was determined to get my college work more or less completed as early as possible, so that I would have time to spend with my family over the holiday period.

Like most teenagers, Ginnette had become a 'gobby' so and so. I did not like her attitude, but at least when she went out she would always tell me where she was going, who she was going with, and she adhered to the time set for her to come home. Just after Christmas of 1989, she went out to a club with her friends, and I had told her to be home by 11.00pm, as she was, after all, only sixteen. By midnight she still hadn't come home and I was getting worried, but eventually, at 1.00am she rolled in with a young lad in tow, who apologized profusely for not getting Ginnette home on time. Although I was extremely annoyed, he had at least brought her home safe and sound. She was smitten with Mark, and when he left, she was full of happiness, and wanted to talk to me about him. He was older than her by four years, and was a 'squaddie' (Recruit) in the Royal Welsh Regiment stationed at Whittington Barracks in Lichfield. I had a mixture of feelings about this, as he was in fact an adult, but she was still a teenager, and no doubt he seemed far more worldly wise and experienced than her.

New year came and went, and in January1990 my college course resumed, and for the first time in ages, I felt that things were going just as they should. Ginnette was happy with Mark, and Karl was in the air cadets and also seeing a young girl named Michelle. We would share some evenings together, and I felt a certain pride in the way my children were progressing, however Mark was putting pressure on Ginnette to dress as a young lady, and not the 'baggy jeaned, baggy jumpered' teenager that she actually was. She started to conform to what he wanted, but then he didn't like it at all when other young men started to look at her. There are those who would say that many girls trap their men into marriages by becoming pregnant, but I believe that in a strange way, it was the other way round in the case of Ginnette and Mark. Ginnette was not on the 'pill', so Michael and I spoke frankly to Mark about Ginnette's age, and of our concerns that HE might just have to be the one who was sensible and take precautions. I told him that I hoped he realized just how besotted with him she was. Ginnette was quite naturally embarrassed that we were talking openly to Mark about such matters, but we needed him to know, and I was always aware that it takes 'two to tango'. I might just as well have talked to a brick wall for all the good it did !!.

By August 1990, I had completed my first year at college, but even more pressure was put on me when I asked Ginnette if she was pregnant. At first she denied it, but the mothers instinct in me told me otherwise. In hind sight, and the way things are today, perhaps I should have been proud that she was going to make us Grandparents, but I was selfish. How could I be happy about it when, deep down, I knew that Mark would not take his responsibility seriously, or stand by her morally. I knew that she would only just be eighteen years old when she gave birth, and that really she should be having fun with her friends. I certainly did not want her to be weighed down by single parenting, simply because Mark was not up to the role of parenthood himself.

So, what should have been a carefree, happy, blooming time for Ginnette, turned into a nightmare for all of us. I wanted to believe that I had taught Ginnette correct morals, but, in my anger towards her, I had forgotten just how I had felt when I first met Michael, her Dad, when I was eighteen and 'raring to go' with him!!. I am ashamed to admit now that she was in the firing line of my anger, and that I reacted in a totally opposite way to what I had always believed in, that anyone is entitled to a first mistake!. I could only see me, me, me!. I had Michael with bad health, I had a mountain of college work, finances were, to say the least, tight, and now I had a daughter who was thoughtlessly going to put an extra strain on our household. I called her all the horrible names that I could think of, in my eyes she was a tart, a whore, a slut, and she had given herself readily to the first one who came along. I was certainly <u>not</u> going to bond with this child, and Ginnette was on her own, she would be soiled goods, and no one else would want her now. The strain on her and me was enormous, and I could feel the anger in me rising daily. Ginnette and I were in constant grid lock, but as well as doing my college work, Michael and I made time to take her for her ante-natal appointments and scans at Good Hope Hospital.

The blow for her, though not so for me, because I had half been expecting it, was when one morning at 2.00am there was a knock at the door. I dragged myself out of bed and down the stairs and peeped through the spy hole in the door, only to see Mark standing there. I had a suspicion as to why he had come at this time in the morning, and as I opened the door, he half-heartedly asked if he could see Ginnette. Although I was fuming, I thought she had a right to see him. Michael asked who it was, and when I told him, he got out of bed and came downstairs, then I woke Ginnette, and told Karl and Stephen to go back to sleep, as everything was OK.

There was no way I was going to leave them downstairs together, as I knew, deep in my heart, that this was the 'cooling off' period, and although I had not forgiven Ginnette for carrying on with the pregnancy, I still wanted to be there to support her when the emotional 'bomb shell' was dropped. When we all sat down, Mark told Ginnette that he could not face the responsibility of going to Hong Kong with his regiment, getting married, and becoming a father. Ginnette was crying, and

I told him that I knew all along he would not stand by her, and as he tried to soft talk his way out of it, he said much how he loved her, so I said to him, 'but not enough to stand by her!', then I added, 'Now just piss off and let her get on with her life!'. And that was it, he left.

Ginnette tried to be strong but she was totally devastated, and even then I could not bring myself to cuddle her. I was just so angry, and I wanted to be left alone, (there I go again, me,me,me!), and yet, deep down I wanted to hug her and tell her that I loved her so very much, that of course I would be there for her, and the unborn baby. My own selfish pride was stopping me, as I felt that this pregnancy was a personal insult towards me and her upbringing. I had been hurt so many times in the past and not taken my anger out on any one, but this was my time. The following Christmas was the saddest of times for Ginnette, she had lost her first true love, and her future was uncertain.

It was1991, and January, February and March came and went, by which time Ginnette had rounded off nicely. She had gone from her petite size 10, to what looked like a size24, and considering how small she had been before her pregnancy, it was amazing

Lollipops, Bubblegum, Death and Lies

to see this huge bump in front of her. At the end of that March Ginnette became eighteen years old, and we managed to scrape enough cash together to take her out for a chinese meal to celebrate. Without any help coming from Mark, other people had helped out in any way that they could to make sure that this little being would not come into the world with nothing. Michael's Mum had knitted a mountain of little clothes and blankets, our next door neighbour had given Ginnette a pushchair/pram, and we had bought her a second hand high chair. Luckily we still had the 'Moses basket' that we had bought for Ginnette when she herself was a baby, it had been stored securely, and would soon be put to use again.

A few days before Ginnette was due to give birth, she popped next door to our adjoining neighbours to ask if Debbie would be a God parent to the baby. When Ginnette came back, she was laughing, and I asked her if all was OK. She said, 'Debbie thought I had gone into labour last night', so I asked her what had made her think that?. Ginnette could hardly contain herself as she told me, 'Debbie said there was a lot of moaning coming from the bedroom!'. Now as it was OUR bedroom that was directly next to theirs, not Ginnette's, I felt myself blush as Ginnette asked, 'What on earth were you and Dad up to last night ?'. I laughed and said with a lie, 'nothing!'.

A few days later Ginnette was admitted to Good Hope hospital, and on Saturday, 20th April, our neighbour took a message for us to say that Ginnette was in labour. Michael drove me straight up to the hospital, and I quickly made my way to the labour ward, but before I even got in there, I could hear the profanities issuing forth from Ginnette's mouth, and it was obvious that she was not too far away from giving birth!!. Then it happened, the head, and then the shoulders emerged, and it was all action stations. By the time the cord was cut, Ginnette was pretty much out of it, and so this tiny bundle was handed to me while the midwife was seeing to Ginnette.

May God forgive me for all the things that I had said to Ginnette, for in my arms lay a gift truly sent from God. Ginnette had named this beautiful little girl Bethen, and she melted my heart completely. She was a marvel to behold, and at that very moment I bonded with her. She looked the image of Mark, and I knew then that it was good riddance to him, as this little girl would definitely be his loss, but our gain. However, Ginnette wanted him to know that he had a daughter, so when

Lollipops, Bubblegum, Death and Lies

she and Bethen eventually came home from hospital, we tried to find out how to contact him. We phoned the Royal Welsh Regiment HQ, and explained that we wanted to get a message to him, but we were told that he had indeed been posted to Hong Kong for two years, and that getting a message to him would not be possible. What a load of rubbish we knew that to be, as in any other words the Army had 'closed ranks'. The only other way to do this was to send a letter to Mark's Mum in Wales, so Ginnette did this, though we didn't hold out much hope of a response. So it was, that our only daughter Ginnette was to join the thousands of other young girls in the ranks of single parenthood.

When this news got about, I had my photograph taken at the college, by the local newspaper, as I was the first Grandmother that the college ever had taking the N.N.E.B. course. The headline was, **'Knitting grandmother completes college course'**, but the ironical thing is that I can neither knit, or sew, I absolutely hate both, and I had not yet completed my course!. It only goes to prove how true it is,...that you can never completely believe anything you read in the newspapers !!.

With examinations coming up, I was

cramming all the hours I could manage into revising, but of course, after taking the exams, and once the course was finished with, for the first time in two years I had time on my hands.

I felt quite awkward applying for jobs, mainly because I could not give a definite answer as to whether or not I had passed the exams and had gained the diploma. One school that I had worked my placement with, asked if I would be able to work for them starting in January 1992. I was told that It would not matter if I had passed or failed, because this was for a full time classroom assistant, and I would be perfect. I had already been police checked, I knew the school regime, and I also knew the clientele that attended the school. Needless to say I jumped at the offer. It did, however, mean that from the July, when I had completed my course, until the January of the following year, I would have no work.

August arrived, and so did my results, I had passed the exams, and I was now a qualified Nursery Nurse. I wasn't proud, but I wasn't unhappy either, it was something that had to be done, and I had done it. When January 1992 arrived, I started working at the local school, where I was employed for eighteen months as a classroom assistant, and I took over the role of 'bread winner' in our family.

During the time that I was employed at this school, Ginnette left home, went on to have two more much loved children, and we grew closer in our relationship again. Karl also got married and went on to have his own daughter, but unfortunately, his first marriage failed. However he went from strength to strength, and when he met his now second wife Lucy, I could not have wished for a more likeable, friendly, funny, bubbly daughter-in-Law.

As for Stephen, I've tried on numerous occasions to raffle him off, offered to give him away, and even offered to pay someone to take him off my hands, but he won't go, so I guess he will be the one to look after me and Michael in our old age. I am collecting the rubber gloves and incontinence pads now.!!

Chapter 28

SAYING GOODBYE YET AGAIN

In August 2002, Michael and I took some friends to the Black Country Museum, near Dudley, but I hadn't turned on my mobile phone. We'd had a lovely day and only when we were on our way home, did I think to switch it on. Almost immediately, the phone rang, and when I answered it, it was Stephen asking if Pamela's husband, Ian, had managed to reach me. I told him no, and that I would try to phone him back, but as I phoned Ian's mobile, it went straight to answer phone, so I was still non the wiser. As we drove back home, I kept thinking that it must be about Elwyne, that she must be in hospital again because she was suffering from emphysema, and had already, that year, been hospitalized because of her condition. On the other hand, because it was Pamela's husband who'd phoned me, it could be Pam

Lollipops, Bubblegum, Death and Lies

who was in hospital, because her physical health had deteriorated so much, she was now in a wheelchair. Whichever one it was there was no point worrying at this stage as we were miles from home, so we took our friends back home first, and then carried on back to our house. I thought of both Pamela and Elwyne, and vowed that as soon as I got through our front door, the first thing that I would do would be to phone Pam's husband. When I eventually got through, I wasn't prepared for the news that Elwyne had died earlier that day. If I only I'd had my mobile phone switched on, but then what could I have done?, perhaps it was fate that made me leave it switched off. I felt the tears burning my eyes, but it was only as I blinked that they began to fall freely down my cheeks, and I felt the need to go and see her.

I asked Ian what had happened, and he told me that Elwyne's younger daughter, Lorraine, had taken Elwyne in the wheelchair, over to the local shopping centre. Not long after they had got there, Elwyne told Lorraine that she wasn't feeling too good, so would Lorraine please phone for an ambulance. There and then, before Lorraine could do anything else, Elwyne had collapsed and died, there was nothing anyone could do, and she was pronounced dead at the scene. Obviously this must have been devastating for Lorraine, and of course Pam. I asked Ian how Pamela was taking it, and he replied that she was heart broken. When I asked if it would be alright for me to go and see Elwyne, he told me that she was at Heartlands hospital, but that I would have to phone them before going. It was too late for me to go that same day, so the following day, Michael drove me to the Heartlands Hospital, which, co-incidentally, is the hospital where both my Dad and Mum had died. Back then, it was called Little Bromwich Isolation hospital, then East Birmingham hospital, and now Heartlands hospital. I had done my crying on the day before, when I had received the news that Elwyne had died, and I vowed that I was going to be strong, but if I really thought that, how wrong I was.

Michael waited outside whilst I was shown into a room, and there lying on a bed, with a white sheet draped over her, was my big sister. I stroked her head and just looked at her face. I was lost for words, but I thought if I waited long enough, she would wake up and then I could start talking to her. I bent down and kissed her forehead, then I asked her to forgive me for taking away the most precious thing in her life, her daughter, Susan. I spoke of that day, and told her that I never intended it to happen. This was the first and only time I ever spoke to Elwyne about Susan. I suppose I was always afraid of opening up old wounds and hurting her by even speaking Susan's name, but here I was telling her how I felt. Then there came more of those bloody tears again, and I felt so pathetic. I told Elwyne to go and find Susan now, to make up for the time lost while she was on earth, to cuddle her, hold her and keep her, never to let her go again. So while mother and daughter were reunited at last, it seemed ironic that only after her death, could I talk to Elwyne about her daughter, and my feelings of guilt for hurting her. I came back out of the room red-eyed and quiet, it had taken it out of me, and going back home in the car, Michael by my side, as usual I kept what I had said to Elwyne to myself. I still wondered though if she had ever truly forgiven me for that day, way back in August 1959.

Before going home, went to see Pamela, and she and I clung onto each other and let our emotions go. She had not long lost her dad, and so the grieving process for her was to be even greater. She told me when the funeral was likely to be, but It would mean that I will have gone back to work after the six week school holiday.

A few days before the funeral was to take place, Pamela phoned me to say that she had contacted a priest, who she had asked to bless Elwyne's small flat, and would Michael and I like to come over for the blessing. We did go, but as I walked into Elwynes flat, I felt such a terrible sense of loss. Pamela and her family, including Lorraine, and Michael and I, stood in the small kitchen, with our hands together in prayer as the priest started his blessing. I couldn't tell you what was being said, I was so wrapped up in my own emotions, and I went into the bathroom so that people would not be too aware of my blubbering. Elwyne had always kept a nice neat home, and her bathroom, where I now stood sobbing, was no exception. I looked at her toothbrush, flannel, and towel neatly placed over the rail, even the little ornaments that she always kept on the shelf were still in place, then I sat on the floor, alone, and remembered the big sister that I would no longer see. Reaching out for the towel, I buried my face into it, stifling the sound of my sobbing.

On the day of the funeral I would have enjoyed the day off work if it hadn't been for such a sad occasion. The cortege made

Lollipops, Bubblegum, Death and Lies

it's way to Witton Cemetery where Elwyne was to be buried, alongside Fred and Susan. Once there, we went inside the church, where there was the usual ritual of prayers, and hymns being sung, but if Elwyne had wanted an angelic chorus, then she was to be very disappointed, as we all sounded like the band of wailers that we were!. Out of the chapel, ready for the burial itself, for the first time in my life I saw the grave in which Susan had been laid to rest. This was especially poignant for me, because I had never been <u>allowed</u> to see her resting place, and even if I had asked my Mum or Dad, they would probably have made some excuse not to take me. Yet the odd thing is that my Aunt Dolly and Uncle Albert, who we used to visit when I was younger, lived directly opposite the cemetery, although at that age I would not have made any connection between the cemetery and their address .

The day was a very sad affair, and an unusual one for me, as although I had been to cremations, this was the first burial that I had ever attended. I felt it was all becoming too much for me. Elwyne was only sixty seven when she died, and I remember thinking, where was her 'three score years and ten'?, or my Mums, or my Dads, or Susan's and

John's, and as for our first born baby, she never even had a stab at life, and I felt robbed and embittered.

I watched through bleary eyes as Elwynes body descended into the ground, and I took stock of Pamela breaking her heart and holding onto her own family. As I watched friends holding handkerchiefs up to their faces, the same question was constantly forming in my mind,...Had Elwyne truly forgiven me?. She might have told Pamela that she had, and that she did not hold me responsible for Susan's death, it was, after all she who asked me on that fateful day, to take Pamela and Susan 'round the block' just one more. But it was me that was there, I was the one pushing the pushchair holding two small children, I was the one, I kept thinking, and surely I could have done something more to avoid what had happened that day. I still felt ultimately responsible for Susan's death, and I could not ever get past that particular obstacle. Neither could I, on the day of the funeral, muster up the curiosity to look at the gravestone which informed people of Susan's dates of her birth and death. I left the cemetery, still none the wiser as to what her epitaph had actually said.

Back at Pamela's house, after the funeral,

the mood lightened, and I tried to smile and join in, but I really wanted to leave, to push things to the back of my mind. I remembered thinking, 'these things are sent to try us, but just how many more 'things' are going to be sent my way?'. I thought, 'My God, I must have been a wicked person in a previous life', after all, in the first twenty one years of my life I had lost a niece, a father, a brother, and just to cap it all, my own precious baby daughter. I felt that I had endured more tragedies than your 'average Joe', but I knew that once we had left Pamela's, tomorrow would be another day, and that I would have to go back to my routine, back to my job, back to being a wife and a mother. I was now beginning to feel angry about life, and I felt the need to find a hill, miles from anywhere, climb to the top, and scream, shout obscenities, thump the air, anything!.

The stress I felt was beginning to mount up, but I might well have calmed down if I could had spoken to a professional counsellor. Once again I never considered seeking advice, because I was not going to let myself down, and the feelings that I was experiencing were my problem, no one else's. Besides which, I was not prepared for someone to judge me, or for that matter my brother, or my family, nor for someone to make light of my situation. I felt that I had coped for all these years without telling, or talking to anyone, so why should I need to seek any help now?.

Chapter 29

MOBILE !!

One other success I had managed to achieve, just after I had gained my N.N.E.B diploma, was to pass my driving test. It made life a little easier for me, as I did not have to rely so much on Michael now to get me to and from work. We had to 'share' the car however, and I had it Monday, Wednesday, and Fridays, and Michael had it the rest of the time.

One day, some years later, in March 2004, I was travelling to work in the car, and I had crossed the white line at a set of green traffic lights, indicating that I was going to turn right. There was another car behind me which had also crossed the white line, also waiting to turn right. As the lights changed, I started to complete my manoeuvre, followed by the car behind me, and It was then that I saw a large white van travelling straight towards me from the opposite direction. The van showed no sign of stopping for the red traffic light that was showing against him, so I slammed on my brakes. It was too late!, he hit the front of my car spinning it around in the opposite direction. My glasses had shot off my face and ended up, somehow or other, in the rear of the car, although luckily, I had put some 'polygrip' on my teeth that morning, otherwise they might have shot through the windscreen!.

Luckily, I had two witnesses who had seen the accident taking place, and The police and ambulance had been called as I was aware of a burning pain in my right shoulder, and a feeling of heavy pressure on my chest. After the ambulance man had examined me, he was convinced that I had wrenched my sternum, and advised me to go to see my own doctor for pain killers. Our Proton car, which we had bought less than a year previously was a 'write off', as when the repairs were assessed, it was found to have more than three thousand pounds worth of damage, far more money than the car was worth!.

I took some time from work, as I was very shook up, and I kept going over and over it in my mind, which would not switch off from the events that had taken place. I was annoyed even more that we no longer had a car, as when I did return to work, It meant that I had to walk the two and a half mile or so there, as well as walking back in the evening. My colleagues had all offered to give me a lift home, but as usual I was too proud to accept. Like all of my other problems, this was just another one to add to the list.

With the police statements completed, we started the insurance claim going, and the police, in the meanwhile, decided to start proceedings to prosecute the van driver. One day some months later, I received a letter saying that the driver of the van, despite me having witnesses, was contesting the charge. He now claimed that the accident was all my fault, which meant that I would have to attend the magistrates court in Burton-on-Trent. This tipped the balance, and from then on I started to panic, I wasn't sleeping, and I was bottling up the true extent of how I was feeling. Then one morning, a few weeks before the court appearance, I cried and told Michael that I couldn't cope with going to court, I had made up my mind I that was not going, and no one was going to make me.

Michael, though he fully understood the reason that I felt like this, tried to explain that I had got to attend by law, but I was still adamant that I was not going, I just was NOT going to go!. I was not going to be shot down in flames again, I was not going to be disbelieved, and I was not going to be made out a liar again. As far as I was concerned, the driver of the van WAS at fault, not me, so what would I do if HE refused to give evidence in court, just as Bob Ward had done all those years ago when I was a child. Would this time be any different, and would I be believed now?. I'd had witnesses back then, and Ward had still gotten away with it, so what then if this van driver convinced the 'bench' that it was me at fault. My mind whirled around and around with the worry of it all.

There was a contact number for a witness liaison officer at the courts, and I decided to telephone them and make an appointment to speak to her. When I entered her office, I thought 'what the hell am I doing here?', but then she shook my hand, and tried to put me at ease, before asking what she could do for me. How was I going to tell a total stranger my reasons for not wanting to go to court?. As I sat down, I faltered, and I told her that I really didn't know where to start, but in my mind I knew that I had to tell her of my past experience in a courtroom, and that she would be first person (apart from Ginnette

Lollipops, Bubblegum, Death and Lies

and Michael), to whom I would relate what had happened to me in 1959. It may well have been forty five years or so earlier, but I can still see that child standing in the 'dock', being made to look a fool in front of all those 'big people'. I could still see the person who'd got away with it, Bob Ward, who I really believed must somehow have managed to bribe the judge, or had been able to pay for a 'smart arse' of a Barrister to swing it his way. There was the verdict of 'Accidental Death', but to me, there should have been another verdict, that of driving recklessly without due care and attention, failing to stop at the scene of an accident, and withholding evidence. So why wasn't 'the book' thrown at him then?.

As I gabbled out the events of August 1959, I became so upset, that I told her that if I had to go to prison for a few days, then I would much rather do that than set foot in any court,(Logic having taken a holiday!). Although she was sympathetic about my feelings, she told me that I really had no say in the matter, and that I had to attend court, but she promised me that on the day, I would be kept apart from the van driver and the witness. She would also take me into the courtroom beforehand to try and ease my reluctance,...Yeah, right!!.

Back at home, my sleeping pattern became worse, and I would wake at 2.00 am, 3.00am, 3.30am, and not be able to get back off to sleep. Then I would get up at 6.30am, shattered, but still ready to start work. I would come home again after work feeling exhausted, and by 9.00pm I would be falling asleep in the chair. I would then try to force myself awake again, thinking, 'If I stay awake just a little bit longer, maybe I will sleep properly until 6.30am'. Unfortunately, it only made matters worse, because then I would become over tired and not be able to settle when I did eventually go to bed. It had became a vicious circle, and the court date was getting closer and closer. My work was beginning to suffer, and I was not concentrating properly on my job, though I hasten to add that the children in the nursery and reception classes didn't ever suffer because of my problems, and I was able to put the forthcoming events on hold until I got home each day.

When the court date arrived, I dressed smartly, and as Ginnette had said that she would come along with Michael and me for moral support, we picked her up on the way there. All the way to the court, I was quiet, and my stomach was doing somersaults. I felt physically sick, my heart was pounding,

Lollipops, Bubblegum, Death and Lies

and my mouth was dry. I knew that I was not going to be believed, even before we had got there, witness or no witness.

As soon as I entered the light airy building, which was not at all like the Birmingham Crown court that I remembered, I felt the anxiety rise, I would not be fooled by the look of the building, it was still a court!. We were then shown into a small waiting room, where there was another person, and It was my witness,...who was nonchalantly eating a sandwich. I said to him, 'I Hope you don't mind me asking, but are you the person who stopped and helped me on the day of the crash', to which he answered, 'yes, I'm your witness', so I thanked him for his help that day. Imagine my surprise then, when he said to me, 'Actually, I feel sorry for him (the driver), you should have seen the state of his van'. My hackles immediately rose, and I ranted at him, 'The state of his van!, it was his fault, he caused £3,300.00 worth of damage to our car, which was a complete write off, and you feel sorry for him?!!'.

Ginnette told me to calm down, and then went to find the witness liaison officer that we had seen previously. When she came in, she moved this man to another room and apologised to me profusely, telling me that it should not have happened, there had been a mistake, and we should have been taken to another room. But the damage had been done now, and it only compounded what I already thought, that no one was going to believe me, and after what he had just said, I believed my witness was going to change his statement and say that it was my fault after all.

The liaison officer brought me a drink, and said that she would be back shortly to show me inside the courtroom,…'Oh Goody Goody!', I thought sarcastically, 'I cant wait, Piss me pink, and all that!'. I was already shaking, and I certainly didn't want to go and see it, but when the time arrived, Ginnette came with me into the actual courtroom itself. It was then as if a grey cloud had descended over the room, as I noticed that everywhere was a mass of highly polished dark brown wood, and a tremendous wash of feelings came over me. I knew that I was not going to cope, I knew that I would breakdown in front of everyone there, and I felt ashamed that I was not strong enough to accept the situation. The witness liaison officer told me, that when I was being questioned, to look straight ahead of me at the 'bench', I was not to worry, and that it would soon be over, but

Lollipops, Bubblegum, Death and Lies

immediately I thought, 'not for me'. Seeing the courtroom hadn't really helped, I'd 'been there, done that, got the t shirt', and It made no difference at all to the way I was feeling or coping. My stomach was knotting up and all I wanted to do was go home, back to my security.

We were taken back to the witness waiting room, and I knew there was nothing more I could do now, except wait, but when the door finally opened, it was a barrister who stood there. He told me that the driver of the van had now admitted it was his fault and had pleaded guilty, and that we would not be called, so we were free to go. I wanted to see that other driver, and call him a bastard for putting me through all the crap that I had endured over the past few weeks, and to ask why had he suddenly decided to come clean?.

It transpired that on the day of the accident, Ginnette and her then husband had gone to where our car was to pick up some of our belongings out of the boot, and the other driver happened to still be waiting by his van. He had approached Ginnette and asked who she was, and was most apologetic when he found out that she was my daughter. He told her that the accident was all his fault, that he had been travelling too fast, and didn't stop at the traffic lights. Ginnette had apparently told this to the witness liaison officer when we had arrived earlier that day, and had asked if she could also be a witness. The barrister had then spoken to Ginnette and asked if she would swear on oath what she had told him, and Ginnette said 'of course she would'. It seems that this had 'got back' to the van driver, and so he had changed his plea at the last minute.

One the way home, although it was early enough for me to return to work, I made the decision to take the rest of the day off, as I could not face the prospect of returning to work after such a strenuous morning. I thanked Ginnette for all she had done, and we dropped her back home. I felt mentally shattered, but that night was the same as it had been for the past few weeks, and I must have woken up three or four times during the night.

We now had the problem of waiting for the insurance claim to be settled before we could buy another car, as well as sorting out physiotherapy for me as my sternum was causing me some problems. At work I couldn't lift any heavy equipment and had to rely on my colleagues, which again I felt dreadfully guilty about doing. I also had to stop working for a while at my part-time second job as a care worker at an old folks home, because I could no longer lift the patients. This eventually resulted in me handing in my notice altogether, as I felt I was letting down the staff by having to refuse the shifts that I was offered. However, I realized that I would become more of a danger than a help to the residents, because I might well have dropped them, if the pain in my sternum 'attacked' at the crucial moment of lifting.

Eight months after the accident and three months after the court episode, I was still not sleeping well, and I was still angry at being taken to court for something that was not my fault, even though my evidence wasn't needed in the end. My mind was racing constantly, and there were times that I found it difficult to take in information, let alone retaining it. Even though I tried hard, I found it difficult to switch off, and even when I tried to relax by reading a book, if I read a passage once, I'd read it a dozen times, and still be none the wiser as to what I had read!. In the end I just gave up.

Chapter 30

Help!!

December 2004 was also a stressful time at school. As well as Christmas parties to organise, there were the cards and calendars that the children had to make for their parents, Christmas concerts to rehearse, 'goodies' to be made for the Christmas Fayre, and still the six areas of learning had to be carried on with. I would return home each evening and console myself that I could look forward to two whole weeks off school for the Christmas holidays. Once the concerts were out of the way, then the time at school really became just a 'fun and wind down' time, with only the children's parties left to enjoy.

With Just a few days to go before the school concert, once the children had gone home, our line manager called a meeting, during which it was decided to tell the parents that we were not going to allow them to video

Lollipops, Bubblegum, Death and Lies

tape the concert this year, and so this was duly noted in the 'minutes'. However, on the day of the concert, our line manager was away from school with a bout of illness. That morning, I was marking the register, as the parents and children came through the door, when one of the parents asked me whether it was alright to take videos at the concert. I apologised, and told her that senior management had decided against it. She in turn told the father of one of the other children, 'No videos'. This man immediately spun on his heels, and in front of all the parents said, 'Why?, and don't give me any crap about the children's protection act!'. Again, I apologised, and told him that I would check with my colleague, so I said, 'Am I correct, that the decision was taken not to allow videos?'. She verified this, and so I told him that it was correct.

He left in a huff, and I thought that was the end of the incident, naively. So we dressed the children in their costumes as quickly as we could, and it was decided that I would narrate the story. By this time however, after dealing with an irate parent, the fun, for me, had been taken away, and I just wanted to get it over and done with. Just before we took the children into the hall, my colleague ran round to the head teachers office and told him what had just taken place with this parent.

Once the children were all ready, I looked through the door leading into the hall, and though the exclamation of, 'Oh Bugger!', doesn't quite fit the feeling, there in the hall were the parents of children in the other key stages at the school, with their video cameras and camcorders merrily filming away. I told my colleague what I'd just seen, but there was nothing for it, but to just get the little ones into the hall, do what we had to do, and face the consequences afterwards!. As the children were led into the hall, bugger me, if this same parent that I had apologised to earlier, was right in my face, and he rudely shouted, 'YOU TOLD ME NO VIDEO'S!'. I could feel my hackles rise, but I knew that I had to remain professional, so I just looked him full on, and said, 'Would you like to speak to the head teacher?'. Luckily, the head teacher was already in the hall, and so he led him away to his office.

The children's little concert itself went very well, however on the way back to the classroom, in front of all the children, one of the parents grabbed my colleagues arm and said, 'You were well out of order telling us there was to be no videos!'. Once the

Lollipops, Bubblegum, Death and Lies

children had got changed and had left for home, my colleague and I were talking, and it transpired that our line manager had fallen ill before having time to let the head teacher know of her decision, but then none of us are infallible.

The following morning, when the parents came through the door, one of them handed me two letters, one was addressed to me, and another to my colleague. It was only once dinner time came, and the morning children had left for home, that I sat down and opened my letter. How kind of this parent!, he was informing us that we were inept at our job, and that he was seeking advice from a solicitor with the view of taking us to court. I felt a 'doolally twot' moment suddenly coming on, Oh my God, I took it so badly!. Why should anyone want to take me to court for doing my job, especially as I was acting on a senior managers decision!.

Once I got home, I told Michael how I felt and showed him the letter, whereupon he told me to just hand in my notice. I became angry, though not with him, and said to him, 'Sod it, they can stick the job up their arses, for £13.000 a year, it isn't worth it!'. There again, I was now the 'bread winner', so I knew I had to be strong, only deep down I knew that I wasn't.

The following day, the head teacher was shown both letters, and he decided to invite the parent in question back into his office. He then apparently told him that it would be his prerogative if he wished to take us to court, but that he should remember that any members of school staff would have the full backing of himself, and of Staffordshire County Council. A short time later, the head sent for my colleague and myself, and when we entered the office, he told us that this parent had decided not to pursue the matter any further. The parent then apologised to us, but all I could bring myself to do was sneer at his apology.

I cannot go into any great detail, but it appears that he was not going to take us to court because he had been sent to live in Tamworth from another county, on a police protection scheme. He had been involved in an armed robbery somewhere in the north of England, and Tamworth was now his home. This meant that to appear in court himself would have apparently put him at some sort of risk of Identification, and therefore of danger to himself and his family!.

I wanted to tell this parent that he was a

Lollipops, Bubblegum, Death and Lies

total idiot, especially when he asked us not to take it out on his child, who was attending the nursery. What did this fool take us for?. I was employed for the well being and education of his child, and for any other children that passed through the door, I wasn't there for the likes of him!. If you can get on with the parents, as well as their children too, it is a bonus, and in the all the time I had been at this school, I had never before encountered a problem like this with any other parent.

As I left the office, I went into the toilets and broke down in tears. This man might well have backed down, but once again, I could not cope with the prospect of his threat of court. I really hated him, but now, to act in a professional manner, I still couldn't have my say!. As I was washing my hands and drying my eyes, the school secretary came into the loo, and she asked what was wrong. I was so full of emotion that I couldn't answer her, I just shook my head and motioned that I was OK, but she told me to go into the staff room, and she would get the head to come and talk to me. I didn't really want her to, but it was too late, she had gone to find him. What the bloody hell was I actually going to tell him?. I really did want to tell him why I was so upset, and I wanted to tell him of my past, but I needed help not sympathy. When he came into the staff room to speak to me, I clammed up and told him that I was just feeling down because of this mans threat. He told me again, that if it had gone to court, I would have had the full backing of the County Council. Unfortunately, because of MY own inability to openly communicate with him, he had totally missed the point.

As the Christmas holiday came and went, I was dreading the day when I had to return to school. I was finding it difficult to cope with most things by now, and I almost envied Michael's ill health because it meant that he could stay in the safety of our home. On the other hand, I felt that I had to persevere both mentally and physically. When January 2005 came, I reluctantly got out of bed, had my shower then breakfasted. I was constantly watching the hands of the clock, and I desperately wished that I did not have to go into work. Once there, I felt that I wanted nothing to do with any of the parents, even though 99% of the parents were really super, and the rapport with them had always been good. I just kept my head down and got on with my work with the children, then I made a decision that I was not there to be liked, I was there to do a job. Gradually I even became distant to my colleagues, and the only ones that mattered to me now on were the children. From now on, as far as I was concerned, the parents were there only to drop them off at the nursery.

My sleeping pattern had become more and more irregular, and I was finding it difficult to rouse myself in the mornings, yet, even when the weekend finally came I couldn't have an extra lay in bed because I found it too difficult to relax. I seemed to be on the go all the time, and I didn't want to go out anywhere, I just wanted to be left alone, and I didn't want to see anyone. If someone had taken me away on an Airplane and dropped me off on some remote island, I wouldn't have cared less, as climbing that metaphorical 'hill' was looking a good prospect. On most days now, at some point, in the privacy of my own home, and away from Michael and Stephen, I would have a good old blubber.

Something happened one day at school, which I would not have normally taken any notice of. It was a community day, where parents were encouraged to come into the nursery/reception and participate in activities with their children, and because it was still winter, it was decided that we would make some 'fat balls' for the birds to feed on. When the children arrived they chose the activity that they wanted to participate in, and I had a group of six or seven children round the table with me. As we were looking at the seeds, and talking about the birds, I was explaining what we were going to do with the fat and the seeds, and how we were going to hang them from the trees for the birds to feed upon. I then put the seeds into a bowl, and when we got to the messy bit, we were up to our elbows in fat and seeds. We were all giggling and saying what it felt like to touch, pulling faces and saying 'yuk', etc., but when my line manager came over to see what we were doing, she quite innocently joked, 'Oh Mrs Brown, you are disgusting!'. This was a remark that I would have laughed off at any other time, but for some reason, I took it badly. Although I did not say anything at the time, when I got home, I replayed her words to me over and over again in my mind. It was then that I realized there was something seriously wrong with the way I was thinking, and I knew the time was fast approaching for me to seek help.

The following day, as I was setting up my activity, I realized that I was silently crying, and that I had to talk to my line manager and tell her how I felt about her comment. I felt

Lollipops, Bubblegum, Death and Lies

pathetically like a teenager who couldn't take any criticism, and even though I knew that it hadn't been meant as an insult, it hadn't been meant to hurt, and it hadn't been meant as a slur on my ability to do the job, that Is exactly the way it felt to me. I was becoming ultra sensitive to absolutely everything, which was very unusual for me, and for the rest of that day, I felt somehow like a victim. I was beginning to resent everything, and, I am ashamed to say, everyone, with the exception of my immediate family, and I felt that work was encroaching on <u>my</u> time and space. I questioned myself again as to why I was even doing this job, as I had reached the stage where I felt that if I couldn't help myself, how then, was I supposed to help these innocent little people who were looking to me for guidance?. My mood was now extremely low, and I had never in my adult life felt quite this way before.

I continued to struggle on in the best way that I could, then one Thursday, one of my colleagues told me that she had a doctors appointment later that morning. So after setting up my own mornings activity ready for the children, I told my colleague that I was going into the 'Knowledge and understanding' room, to set up her activity ready for when she came back from the doctors. As I sat down preparing the things needed for that particular activity, I suddenly lost it completely, my tears were staining the papers that I had been preparing, and I needed to get away. I knew that I had a duty to the children in our care, but I also knew that at this particular time, I was not capable of doing it. I felt that I would be letting those children down, as well as the people that I worked with, and so a vicious circle seemed to be tightening round me. My line manager then appeared at the door, and two words were all it took, as she asked, 'what's wrong?', so I told her that I was not coping with things. But as I still could not explain to her what those 'things' were, she, along with my other colleagues thought that I was just referring to my work. How wrong they all were, my conscientious feelings towards my job were only weighing so heavy on my mind because of the other long hidden problems, those were the 'things' that I could no longer cope with!.

She told me that it would be best to go home and make a doctors appointment, but how I got home is anyone's guess, as when I did get into the car I was practically blinded by my tears. I felt that this was so stupid, and I asked myself, 'what can a

Lollipops, Bubblegum, Death and Lies

doctor possibly do for me, can he take away my past, can he make me feel better about myself, can he bring Susan, Elwyne, Mum or Dad back?', because those were the things that I wanted. This time I never even spared a thought for John, Sod that!. Michael was surprised to see me when I opened the front door. He asked me what had happened, and I managed to tell him that I had been sent home, and that I needed to make a doctors appointment. Although I couldn't explain to him why I needed to see the doctor, I think that somehow, Michael already knew.

I picked up the phone and dialled the number, but as I was speaking, I realized that I was inexplicably shaking and stuttering. I left it until the last minute before travelling to the doctors for the 11.15 am appointment I had been given, and as I entered the health centre, I felt that everyone was looking at me, and that they knew all my secrets. Bloody hell, now I really was becoming paranoid!. I sat alone in a corner hoping that no one would notice me whilst I was waiting for my name to be called, but when I was called, it was by a doctor that I had not seen there before. With my eyes cast downwards, I entered his consulting room, and he then asked what he could do for me, but I just sat there, knowing that the moment I opened my mouth, the tears would flow freely. What the hell was wrong with me?. The big question on my mind was, 'why now was my past haunting me, why now!, Why?.

The doctor was quietly spoken, and patient enough to wait for my response, but when it finally came it was like a barrage of garbled words. I told him that I could not cope with anything at all, and I found myself telling him about the accident involving Susan, to which he listened intently as I sobbed out everything that had happened that day. My heart was racing again, and I felt yet another rush of guilt wash over me. What rights did I have to tell anyone what had happened to that poor little girl, and did I really want anyone to know that it was my fault that she had died?. The doctor continued to listen patiently, and three quarters of an hour later I left his room with a note exempting me from work for one week. Although he did not prescribe any anti-depressants, he asked me to make an appointment for the following week, to see how I was coping.

I took the note into the office at work and then made a hurried escape, just wanting to get back to the safety of my own home as soon as I possibly could. I could only just cope with one day at a time, so to wait a week seemed like an eternity to me. If the phone rang I got Michael to answer it, and if anyone knocked on the door, again, Michael had to answer it, and I avoided any possible contact with anyone at all. As far as I was concerned, the world could end there and then, and I wouldn't have given two hoots, provided that I had my family with me.

That night I went to bed feeling extremely tired, but the moment that my head hit the pillow, I was wide awake again, and I just lay there wishing that sleep would take a hold on my body, hoping that I would wake in the morning feeling refreshed. As I lay there, I could see past events, and I could hear harsh words that had been said to me over the years. I wished that I was someone else, someone who was confident, someone who'd had a carefree childhood, and as I lay listening to the tick of the clock, I tossed and turned, closing my eyes only for them to 'jump' open again. Then I thought, 'this is it, the thing that I'd vowed all those years ago would never happen to me, was actually happening, I was going 'doolally twot', I was having a mental breakdown!!.

Because I was not sleeping through the night, by the following morning I couldn't rouse myself either, and because I had slept in later than was normal for me, by bed time I wasn't ready for sleep either. I found myself lying there awake until one or two o'clock in the morning, and then what sleep I did get would be disturbed by my thoughts. I was becoming more and more lethargic with each day.

The following Thursday, when I went back to see the same doctor, I told him that after being off work for a week, I really ought to think about going back, but he disagreed, and said that he was not prepared to state that I should return to work just yet. He then asked me if I thought I needed to see someone for counselling, but I told him no, as to me that would only confirm that I was 'off my perch', and I have believed all along, that my problems were mine to deal with, they were no-one else's.

After this had gone on for about a month, I found that I could no longer retain information. It was as if my mind had begun to shut down, and I was becoming more and more agitated, so I reluctantly had to face the fact that I needed to seek advice after all. When I went back to the doctors yet again, I lowered my pride and asked if he could refer me to someone who could help me, so he told me that he would start the process of referral immediately. It wasn't too long before I heard from the mental health authority. I went along for an initial assessment, and when that had been completed, I just had to wait for an appointment to come through to see a community psychiatric nurse.

Chapter 31

LEARNING TO LIVE WITH IT

Some friends of ours, Margaret and Phil who lived in Redditch, phoned me up for a chat, as we didn't get to see each other very often. They had bought the chalet off Michaels Mum and Dad a couple of years earlier, because Dunster Beach was loved by her family, as well as ours. As we talked, I told her that I was having some problems with my health, that I was off work, and of how I was feeling so low, and so sad, but just couldn't put my finger on why. A couple of days later, the phone rang, and It was Margaret, who told me that she and Phil had been talking, and they would like to know if we would care to spend a few days at the chalet, as an early birthday present?. I didn't need asking twice as this could be the break that I needed, away from any stress, being able to do what I wanted to in my own time,

Lollipops, Bubblegum, Death and Lies

with nothing to worry about for the next few days. So thanking her and Phil, I put the phone down, then told Michael about their generous gift to me.

A few days later, after putting a few clothes into a suitcase, and buying some extra food to take down to the chalet with us, Michael, Stephen and I travelled down to Somerset. We always knew that we were near our destination, as soon as we caught sight of the 'Ogres Castle' on the hill at Dunster. It had become a traditional landmark that even the youngest children immediately recognised, throughout every generation of our family that had holidayed at the chalet. Very soon, as we turned off the A38, and down the lane that led to Dunster Beach, I felt strangely more relaxed, and as we entered the main gate, with the sea in view to my right, I was at peace. We drove along the road to the chalet, number 257, and I took in all of the sights that had become so familiar to us over the years, and when we actually reached it, I got out of the car as excited as a child!. I put the key into the lock, opened the door and sniffed, the chalet always had a smell to it that seemed familiarly warm and welcoming, and somehow stuffed full of nostalgia and fond memories.

We brought the cases in, put on the kettle, and had our drinks of tea and coffee. I was so grateful to Margaret and Phil, and I knew, that by letting us have the chalet for the week, they were in fact, losing money. We had a wonderful 'chill out' week, sometimes just walking along the quiet beach, huddled up in our coats. The night times were spent in the soft glow of the chalet lights, but although I had taken some books to read, I still found it too hard to concentrate, so It was easier to be entertained by watching the television. The mornings were still heralded by the quacking of the ducks outside the chalet, demanding their traditional rations of dry bread!. We didn't really feel the need to go anywhere except to Dunster itself, where I took the opportunity to point out to Stephen the hotel that he, Ginnette, Karl had paid for us to stay in when we celebrated our thirtieth wedding anniversary. We did go into Minehead just for a bit of shopping, but apart from that, we were happy with our surroundings, the familiar soft rustling of the wind through the trees outside, and our wonderful nostalgic memories.

We knew that Margaret and Phil were coming down to the chalet themselves on the following week, and that some of their family

Lollipops, Bubblegum, Death and Lies

were going to join them on the Monday. As the week progressed, I received a phone call from Margaret to ask if everything was OK, and Michael suggested that I asked if they wanted to come down to the chalet earlier, as it was, after all, their chalet. When I asked her, she answered 'No, we don't want to spoil your holiday'. How kind was this of them?. But, of course, I really did want to see our friends, who in truth, were the only people, outside of my immediate family, that I always looked forward to seeing. So on the Friday, Margaret and Phil arrived with 'Cessie', their old dog, and although I was excited about seeing them, I wondered what they would see in me. We hugged each other, and talked while they settled in, and although it was their chalet they didn't take over. We spent the evening drinking wine, (I had a rum and coke!), and we ate chocolates,...it was the perfect evening in!!.

This was probably the first time that I had felt able to laugh out aloud for many months. The chalet had three single beds and one double bed, and even then they told us to have the double bed, as they would happily sleep in one of the singles. As we all settled down, I could hear Margaret and Phil giggling, because the single bed really was too small for the two of them, so they were having fun, of sorts, trying to find a way of actually staying in it!. As if that wasn't bad enough, Michael, who was the first to fall asleep, then started snoring,...loudly!, and with no exaggeration, it was like having a wailing banshee in the room with us!. I apologised to Margaret and Phil for the snoring, and I heard Margaret and Phil laughing, 'Good God!, do you have to put up with this every night?', she asked. When the snoring did stop and it went quiet, Margaret asked if Michael had died, and said that It might better to hear him to snoring again, just to be on the safe side!. This snoring went on most of the night, so needless to say, on the following morning, Michael received some good natured stick off all of us, including Stephen, who suggested that I placed a pillow over his Dad's head the next time!.

As we all sat round the table having breakfast and talking, Margaret asked me if I wanted to go for a walk while the men washed up, seeing as we had made the breakfast. It sounded like a good enough idea to me!. Margaret and I cut through the chalets on the front row, and stumbled over the pebbles that lead down onto the beach, and although the wind was blowing, it wasn't freezing cold.

As we strolled along, she asked if we'd had a nice time, and I told her how I appreciated her thoughtfulness. Yes, of course we'd had a smashing time, as it was a much needed break that had come at just the right time. Then, I told her why I had been off work for such a long time, and that I was waiting to see a psychiatric nurse. She wasn't shocked, she just let me do the talking, and for some reason that is exactly what I did. She did tell me that if I did not want to talk about it, then that was fine, but if I did want to, then she would be happy to listen. So, I proceeded to tell her of my feelings of guilt at Susan's death, and I even told her about my brother, John, and that I had never told anyone about my 'problems' with him. We had a long walk that took almost two hours, but within that two hours, Margaret had heard my darkest secrets, and yet I did not feel any threat of losing her friendship. She didn't judge me, she didn't ridicule me for my feelings, and she didn't treat me as a 'nut case'. She had just done as she said she would, she listened.

When I had finished talking, I felt that a weight had been lifted off my shoulders, and I thought that perhaps being at a place that was common to both of us, and that we both had a love for, made it easier for me to open up my thoughts. Another thing that I feel may of helped, was that because Margaret was to some degree, one step 'removed' from my emotions, she could perhaps 'distance' herself a little bit, and see things more objectively and without bias. Whatever the reason, I was grateful to her just for being there at the right time.

That night though was different, and as we all settled down, the inability to sleep started and I felt guilty all over again for letting out the darkest of my secrets. Perhaps I should have talked only of how I was feeling about Susan. I had, after all, vowed that I would never tell a soul about John, and that I would take this secret to my grave. But, it was too late, I had talked, and as with most regretful events in my life I could not turn back the hands of the clock. Then I remembered something, that one evening, in our bedroom back at home in Hebden, before going to work canvassing, I had already told Michael about John, though not in any great detail, as I had with Margaret. There was no point at all in worrying about it now, but I suddenly realised how desperately I needed to talk, and that process was just beginning for me.

On the Sunday, when it was time for us to leave Margaret and Phil to their peace and quiet, before their family joined them at the chalet, we hugged each other and I thanked her for listening, and for, as far as I was concerned, doing the right thing for me at the right time. On the way home there was a mixture of emotions, as I was still feeling low, but I knew that the break had done me a lot of good. I knew that once we got home again the routine would have to recommence, and I knew that I was in for a long talking, healing process ahead.

Not too long after that wonderful break, Margaret and Phil left Redditch and went to live in Watchet, which not very far from the chalets at Dunster, and we all still keep in touch on a regular basis. They often invite us down to stay with them for a few days, or even weeks, months at a stretch!!.... but I don't think even THEY could put up with Michael's snoring for that amount of time!!.

Chapter 32

LEARNING TO TALK ABOUT IT

I went into the room and the community psychiatric nurse introduced herself as Jane. She was completely relaxed, whereas I, on the other hand, was not!. What on earth had possessed me to come here?.

After talking for a little while to get to know me, and how I was feeling, she used an analogy, in telling me what was going to happen. My mind, she told me, was like a big toy box, and the time had come for me to de-clutter, so I was going to keep the good toys, and throw out the old ones, and when I was ready, she was going to help me. I still felt so sad, and I couldn't talk at first, as I had the old familiar feeling of my mouth being dry, then I told her, that whatever I was about to relate to her, I did not want her to be judgemental, but she assured me that she was not there for that reason.

When I sat in the chair and started to tell her about Susan, Pamela, and me, it started me off reliving that day again in August 1959, and to say that I became distressed would be an major under statement. My leg was shaking ten to the dozen, and I was wringing my hands to the point where it felt like a chinese burn. She handed me the box of tissues to wipe my eyes, and It took the whole one hour session to tell her in detail what had happened to me, from the time of Susans accident, up to the events of more recent times. She listened patiently and not once butted in, and at the end of the session she asked me how I felt. I told her that I felt as though I had betrayed Susan and myself for talking about it, as It was, after all, an alien concept for me to me to talk about MY problems. Although I had talked about Mum and Dad, and Susan and Elwyne, I had not once mentioned John, as I wanted to keep him hidden in the murky depths of my mind. I really was not going to talk about him, and I felt there was no need to now, because I had already opened up to Margaret. As I left her room armed with my appointment for the following week, I felt both relief and disappointment. I also felt quite confused, because I was now talking openly after all these years.

As I drove home an immense pressure seemed to be building in my stomach, and I could feel the knotting taking a hold, there were tears were blurring my vision, and only when I blinked, did those tears fall away. By the time I managed to get to the safety of home, I was totally exhausted, and when Michael asked me how it had gone, all I could say was, 'OK, got to see her next week'. I'd done my talking for that day, and I just lay down on the settee and fell asleep.

On the following week's visit to Jane, I told her that there was one more secret I needed to tell her about. But, what was I going to tell her?. I did not want her to think badly of me, or my brother, and I did not want her to judge him or me. I broke down in tears yet again as I told her about John, and of the occasions that he had put his hand in my knickers, or down my pyjamas. Then of how I felt so ridged with fear when he had his 'way' with me, that my body would shake, and how he thought that it was because I was cold. How I never could find a way to explain to him that HE was causing me shake with fright. I told her about his 'dares with death', and how I hated him for putting Mum and Dad

Lollipops, Bubblegum, Death and Lies

through all the pain and worry because of his stupidity. My Mum and Dad didn't deserve that!. I told her how I used to cry silently in the bathroom, because in there, I could let the tap run and people would not hear my sobbing. I told her of the incident with the ouija board, and of my walking the estate looking for him that same night. As I parted with all the crap that had happened to me over the years, the one thing I really wanted to know now was, 'Why now, why had all this pain surfaced now?'.

Jane then told me about Post Traumatic Stress Disorders, and how even now, nearly seventy years after the Second World War, those poor people who lived through it were suddenly bringing terrible memories to the surface about events that had happened all those years ago. One theory goes, she told me, that sometimes when things happen to a child, that child will get on with the process of growing up, and they will hide away the distress caused until they reach a more secure time later in life, to let go. Jane suggested that perhaps that time had come for me, and now it was time to let it all go. This made a lot of sense to me, and one thing that really knocked me for six, was when she asked what my job was. I told her that I worked as a nursery nurse at a local school, working with children aged three to five years old. She then asked me how long I had worked with that age group, and I told her it had been fourteen years. She looked thoughtful, as if to question herself as to whether or not to say anything to me, but then said, 'Three to five year olds, for fourteen years, has it ever occurred to you that you have subconsciously served your sentence?'.

The penny still didn't drop, but then she explained. With my qualifications, I could have worked with children aged nought to eight, but instead I had chosen to work with children who were, in fact, the same ages that Pamela and Susan had been at the time of the accident. I was still confused, but yes, if I had chosen to blame myself, because that is what I had been led to believe was true, I had indeed 'served my time'!. It might also go some way to explain why I have such a fear of the courtroom, and how I don't want to serve any more time there. In the whole of the next twelve months of seeing Jane, as well as attending our local mental health hospital for group therapy sessions, I had opened up as much as I possibly could, and the counselling sessions with Jane were to continue for some time yet.

Lollipops, Bubblegum, Death and Lies

On my second course of counselling, I told Jane of my efforts to obtain the High court transcripts, and of my anger at being told of their destruction. I was feeling angry at most things at this stage, from the most trivial of negative things such as, I was sick of the rain each day, people having holidays that we could not afford, lack of cash, blonde bimbo's in sports cars, to even hearing about people living to be in their 80's or 90's, because all of the people that were close to me had not even had, to quote the Bible, their three score years and ten. Then there was the anger I was generally feeling about the fact that I had worked so hard, but I was reaping nothing in the way of rewards. I really could not put my finger on just what I was after, and again I was confused.

One Day, I decided to visit Pamela, who was suffering bad health herself, and by now was more or less confined to a wheel chair. Pamela was very shaky, so I knew that it was a bad day ,health wise, for her. However, while her daughter Nicola made us a drink, I told Pamela, that because of my own health problems, I was now seeing a psychiatric nurse for therapy. She asked me if it was because of my involvement with our mutual past events, but I told her, without disclosing anything else, that there was more to it than that. Pamela then told me that when Elwyne had died, and they were clearing out her flat, she had come across a box in which was a letter from the school that Susan had attended, some newspaper cuttings, a ring, and one or two other little things. She asked if I wanted to see them, as she thought it might help, so I pondered for awhile then told Pamela, that if it didn't upset her, then yes, I would welcome the chance to see these things.

She asked her Nicola to bring the down the box, which was no bigger than a shoe box, which she then handed to Pamela, and as I waited for Pamela to open it, she asked me again if I was sure that I wanted to see the items that it contained. I assured her that I did, but it was like expecting an explosion to occur, and I suppose metaphorically, that that is exactly what happened. The first thing she took out of the box was a letter from the head teacher of Susan's school, offering their condolences to her family. Then there were some old black and white photographs of Susan, and as I looked at them, there was this little blonde girl staring back at me for the first time in forty six years, her hair long and wavy, just as I remembered it on the day she died, and I could really feel my heart strings tugging now!.

Pamela then took out all of the newspaper cuttings that Elwyne and Fred had kept, announcing that there had been an accident in which a five year old girl had died, (their daughter, Pamela's older sister, and my first niece), and as I sat on Pamela's bed in the living room, and started to read the reports, my heart leapt!.

I honestly had always thought that there was only one person in the lorry that day. As I mentioned earlier in this story, on that day I heard a rumble, and on turning my head I saw a lorry approaching, but then I must subconsciously have cast my eyes on the driver, and registered nothing else. As I read on, the whole thing seemed to me, to be making a mockery of my memories. There were two people in the lorry, and Bob Ward had refused to give evidence, so what happened to the other person, and why was he not called to give evidence?. Both my name and address had been published, though Bob Ward got away with just his name being recorded. Then there was John Hathaway, who had eventually admitted that he had lied to the police because he thought that the accident was not as serious as it actually was. They were his own words, 'I was trying to help Mr Ward'. What about the help for me, and for Susan, didn't she need Justice?, whether it was a serious accident or not, he should still have told the truth.

As I read on, I was becoming more and more angry. What had happened to the evidence regarding the maroon paint marks and white rubber marks, on Bob Ward's lorry, and the blatant lie that those marks were old ones?. Had he rubbed them off to get rid of any incriminating evidence?. These 'Adults' were all willing to let a nine year old child to carry the blame for life, as long as it meant that they could save their own arses for one day!!.

I could only bring myself to say one word, 'Bastards'. My mind was raging now, and I cursed them, 'I hope you are all rotting in fucking hell!'. My niece had died that day, and as far as I could see now, the subsequent investigations into her death had descended into a farce. It seems that Bob Ward apparently had a right not to give evidence, but far more important, surely, was Susan's right to life. I still believed that it was Bob Ward who killed her, but that bastard had got away with it. If the outcome was down to a good barrister, then how much did Bob Ward have to pay

Lollipops, Bubblegum, Death and Lies

him to influence that outcome?. I am so glad that Elwyne had the presence of mind to keep hold of these newspaper cuttings, and that Pamela was willing to show them to me, but by God, I was fuming now!.

I asked Pamela if I could hold on to the cuttings so that I could photocopy them, and she gave me her blessing to do so. It was just then that I wanted to ask Pamela a question. I desperately needed to know what SHE thought of me, and I needed to know whether or not she had forgiven me for what had happened, as not only was she injured on that day, but she had lost her sister too. I really needed to know her answers, and I thought that I was prepared for any answer she would give me.

Her response was that she didn't really remember anything at all about the accident, then looking at me she added, 'You are the big sister I never had'. I felt humbled by her answer, and then she added, 'You know, Mum never blamed you for that day, she always said that if she hadn't asked you to take us round the block again, then perhaps Susan would still be here'. Although I said nothing to Pamela at that moment, I still wondered why I found it so hard to accept what she had just said to me. I did, however, accept the compliment paid, that Pamela thought of me as her big sister, so we hugged each other, and then it was Pamela's turn to have a cry. Nicola, bless her, then used a phrase that is routinely uttered in the TV soap 'Eastenders', by characters like Dot Cotton, or Pauline Fowler,...as she said, 'I'll go and put the kettle on then'!.

We then got onto the subject of John, as I was now willing to tell her about him. She then told me that she remembered one time, being in her garden, when she was a little girl, that John was straddling her and tickling her, and that suddenly, her mum had opened the window and shouted at John to get off her.

Pam then said to me, 'I wonder if Mum had any suspicion about John?'. It might seem a bit selfish of me, but if Elwyne did have any suspicion back then, I wished that she would have told me, as perhaps then I might have been able to confide in her. But no, I don't suppose for a moment I would have done. It may be difficult to believe, but at the time of this incident with Pamela, John must have been at least twenty, or twenty one years old. I told Pamela that I had felt sorry for John at the time, because there was obviously a big problem with him, mentally, and he should have received appropriate treatment much earlier than he did. Of course, back in the 1960's, there wasn't the type of help that is available today, so we'll never know.

When I looked over at Pamela, I noticed that she too was getting upset again, so after another drink, we hugged each other and I left for home. As I drove along, my mind was still churning over what I had just read. There had been no justice for Susan, or me for that matter, and I was never going to get to the bottom of this without a court transcript, so that I could see exactly what had been said. Unfortunately, I was still not retaining information in my head, I was a stuttering, blithering idiot on the telephone, and I still didn't really want to speak to friends or colleagues, let alone anyone in authority. If I wanted to seek out those court transcripts, it was going to have to wait until I felt a little more confident.

Chapter 33

BLEAK TIMES, YET MORE REVELATIONS

Over that weekend, I was subdued, and as usual I didn't want to go out, I didn't want to see anyone, and I didn't want to talk to anyone. I just kept on studying the cuttings, and my face was burning with anger. There were two people in that cab after all, two, and at least one of those pathetic excuses for a man, one of those bastards knew the truth. Oh my God!, I can't put into words just how let down, and how incredibly angry I was feeling. That 'hill' was looking more inviting by the day, as up there I could shout the foulest of words without anyone hearing me, and I could curse, and let out all the anger that I was feeling!. The only trouble was, that I knew I could not even muster up the energy to go and find that hill, let alone climb up it, for now anyway.

Lollipops, Bubblegum, Death and Lies

The following week, I kept my appointment with Jane, and after the usual pleasantries I told her how I was feeling, and the reasons for my renewed anxiety. I then showed her the newspaper cuttings, and as she read, I started crying again. What could she say, or do?, nothing,as far as I was concerned!. I wanted to bring Susan back, and I was feeling stubborn about it to the point of telling myself, again, that my imparting of these memories to Jane was just a total waste of time. My problems should be overcome by me alone not by anyone else, yet I knew, in order to help myself, that I had to keep going to counselling, as it was either that, or go 'round the bend' completely!.

As I left that session, and before I went home, I needed to go to the local shop for one or two items, but when I pulled up on the car park, I just sat there, and realised that I could not face going into the store. So I just sat and watched for awhile as people were coming and going, without a care in the world, as it looked to me, and I envied them, what could they know about life?. 'Stuff the shopping', I thought to myself, then started the car and drove home. That day was the first time I felt as though I could not cope with going into a shop or a crowded place on my own, a feeling that remained with me for three more years. From then on I had to rely upon either Ginnette, Stephen, or Michael to come with me, and believe me it became very time consuming, not only for me, but also, of course, for those I needed to rely upon.

Of all the times that I needed someone with me for support and a feeling of security, the worst time was the approach of Christmas. There were to be no surprises for my family that year, as one or the other of them was usually with me. I couldn't even think clearly about the items that I needed to buy in for the Christmas lunch, let alone think about gifts. Up until now I had always loved Christmas. I loved the whole meaning, the true meaning, and I loved having the family together, seeing the faces of my grandchildren as they opened their surprise gifts. I loved setting the Christmas table, complete with 'gift bags' for each of us, listening to the rows, the laughter, and carols being sung, but this time I just could not muster up any enthusiasm at all. Even when each of my children asked me what I would like for Christmas, I would just reply unenthusiastically, 'nothing, thanks'.

Jane was an excellent psychiatric nurse, but I still held back from letting my true feelings out. There were many times at these

Lollipops, Bubblegum, Death and Lies

sessions when I wanted to swear and let out the anguish I was feeling, but I respected Jane and knew that she was not the one I should take out my frustration on. There was only one time that I felt that she doubted me, and that was when I told her about the time I had the still birth. I had told her about the nurse who had brought in the new baby who was about to go home with its parents, and her asking me if I wanted to see a baby!. Jane had asked me, as if I had the answer, 'why would she want to do that?', so because of the delicate state of my mind, I immediately thought, 'here we go again, now she doesn't believe me!'. Now, three years on from those sessions, I realise that she must have seen it as incredulous that anyone could have been so insensitive to the feelings of others. Especially toward someone who, after feeling the baby's movement inside, and even forming a bond with the unborn child, had just given birth but then had no baby to show for the nine months of pregnancy,

I was always happy enough to see my immediate family, but I just could not cope with the thought of seeing other people, so when any of my work colleagues called round to see how I was, I felt uneasy and uncomfortable. I was very conscious of the amount of time they were staying in my domain, and I didn't like their intrusion. My head would shake, my arms and legs felt tense, and their well intended conversations meant very little to me, as I simply didn't want to listen to what they had to say. I didn't want to engage in their social chit-chat, as the conversation always seemed to drift towards the 'goings on' at work, and the last thing I wanted to hear about was work!. I was so wrapped up in my own problems, that the thought of the one particular person, who had presented me with the threat of court action for doing my job, would immediately come into my mind as soon as work was mentioned. In the past I'd always had a good laugh and felt happy working with these colleagues, but now, they too were simply a reminder of the pressures that I would have to face when the time came for me to go back to work, and that thought still terrified me. Needless to say, I was always happy to see my intrusive visitors leave.

I now accepted that I could not cope with my own problems, so how on earth would I cope with the problems presented by little children in a school environment. They deserved far better than I could give to them at this stage in my life. The council departments in charge

Lollipops, Bubblegum, Death and Lies

of the schools were excellent, they kept me informed of any decisions that were made regarding my absence from work, and a representative from the county council came along with the head teacher came to visit me. They eventually arranged an appointment for me to go and see an independent doctor, who was engaged by the council, which of course meant that I also had to tell her everything that was going on, and why. Needless to say, the pressure of having to yet again tell someone else about my past exhausted me, but I realised that it had to be done.

I was by now also attending meetings at the local hospital, along with other people who were either depressed, anxious, or suffering from stress. What that did do, was help me to realise that I was certainly not on my own as far as not being able to cope with life was concerned. Yes, I was depressed, but I was certainly not mad!. There were times at these sessions that I felt that it all got too much for me, mainly because we were all encouraged to talk to one another openly, and I have always felt awkward talking in a crowd. I was fine on a one to one basis with Jane, as if I cried, it was only in front of her, but at the hospital it was different and If I did feel that way, I would have to go into the toilet, get it out of my system, then rejoin the group again, always hoping that no one would notice my red eyes!!. We were also taught relaxation techniques, which I never did get the hang of, and even now I find it terribly hard to relax. It think it takes a lot of courage to close your eyes in a room full of comparative strangers, listen to a relaxation tape, and just drift away. I was constantly aware that I was not alone in the room, and I don't know whether I expected someone to shout, 'Boo!', once we were all settled in a relaxed state, or what?. I just know that these techniques were beyond me then, and perhaps they always will be!.

In the meanwhile, Margaret had got in touch again, as by this time they had managed to buy their own house in Watchet, Somerset, and had invited us to go and stay with them for a few days. While we were there, she asked me how things were going, and again I found it so easy to talk to her, though all the time we were talking I could feel my tummy tightening. This time, I told her that I felt sorry for John because he obviously did not know what he was doing, but though she usually made a lot of sense when we were talking, this time I was shocked when she said to me, 'I think that he knew full well what he was doing'. She was talking in a soft serious voice, and I felt somewhat puzzled by her remark. I had always defended his actions because I believed that he had a problem. She then said, 'If he didn't take away your virginity by his actions, then if anything had been said to your parents, a teacher, or who ever, there would have been no proof of it, but If he had taken it away before you were sixteen years old, the proof would be there, and there would have been serious repercussions for him'. 'Or', she went on, 'he knew that once you reached adulthood, you might have sought justice for yourself, and so, if he was no longer around because he'd taken his own life, he couldn't be held responsible for his actions'.

Wow!, I had never thought of it that way, but If John had still been alive, would I, or could I have gone to the Police and told them of my incestuous affair with my brother over forty years ago?. I don't think I could have, as firstly, I have no proof now, secondly, I was, and I still am, a very loyal person, and thirdly, I could not bear the thought of being laughed out of the police station for wasting police time. So no, I would have to pass on that, as far as seeking Justice goes. I did however tell Margaret ,that although I found my counselling sessions quite exhausting and sometimes very painful, if nothing else, I could at least talk about the past now, without feeling too much guilt.

Now that my mind has been focused on John again, I do wonder, when I think back to the things that he did to me, and the episode with Pamela in Elwyne's garden, if he had the tendencies to go on to become a paedophile, even though I know it is a harsh thing to think or say. I wonder also, if someone is born a paedophile, or whether circumstances predict that that is what you will become. John had, after all been sexually assaulted by a grown man, when John himself was just a child. Perhaps, like me, he could not talk to anyone about his past, as sensitive subjects were generally swept under the carpet in our house. Was he still battling with his feelings, and is that what led him to take his own life?. These are the questions that I know can never be answered, and I have to accept that fact, though with the help that I have received, I think that I can now.

The few days spent with Margaret and Phil were, as usual, very relaxing. We would go into Minehead or Taunton during the day and just potter round the shops, and Margaret and I would usually have a giggle over something or other. As usual being the tight arses that we were, we didn't spend much money, as we never had a lot to spare in the first place!. Again, our evenings were spent relaxing, talking and watching television, together with a few drinks and some chocolates or crisps, so what more could anyone ask for?. These were the simple pleasures in life, the pleasure of good company, of no one asking anything of you, of being accepted for who you are, and not what you can offer in return, and we were grateful for that at least.

Back home again, the half-expected letter from the County Council had arrived, informing me of their decision to allow me to retire on ill health grounds. Although this was a great weight off my mind, I couldn't help but think that this was a final confirmation that I was useless!. Deep down I knew that I still wasn't well, and that in my delicate state of mind I was still very sensitive, and still not able to cope. So that was that, I could now look upon myself as a 'lady of leisure'. Now, if only I could learn to enjoy the time it allowed me, because despite this new situation, I was still not happy going out anywhere. If I knew I had got to go out, even with the support of Michael, or Ginnette, then I had to go, but as soon as I was out, I wanted to get back home again as soon as I possibly could, as I still felt so very much out of my depth out in public.

I always kept in touch by telephone with Doreen and Jean, my two sisters who lived in Canada. They were both making plans to come over to England for a months vacation, and the idea was for them to stay with Karl and his then wife. I was really happy that they were coming over, but I wondered why they were not coming to stay with Michael and me, so I felt compelled that the next time we spoke, I would ask them. Sure enough, during our next telephone conversation, I tentatively asked Doreen to humour me as to why they were they not staying with us. She said that they did not want to put any pressure on me at this time, and so thought that it would make it easier for me if they stayed with Karl. I told Doreen that I would much rather that they stay with us, after all, I was at a selfish stage of my illness, and I had not seen them for a number of years, so It was settled, they would be coming to stay with me and Michael in the February. With certain reservations about what they would think of me, I couldn't wait to see them again.

I loved having my 'big' sisters in our house, all to myself. They knew that I was having some health problems, and so put no pressure on me at all. We were all happy to just relax with a cup of coffee and a book or magazine, or generally 'chit-chat', and to talk of the times when we were younger. They were happy for me to stay at home whilst they went to 'explore' Tamworth or Lichfield, but the offer was always there if I did want to go out with them, and whatever I wanted to do, they would quite happily go along with it.

One night, when Michael had gone up to bed before me, as I went to kiss Doreen and Jean 'Goodnight', they both took my hands in each of theirs, and in a serious tone asked how I was <u>really</u> doing. I nodded my head and said 'good', but obviously they could see beyond that. Doreen then asked me a strange question, 'Is any of this to do with John?'. I was quite taken aback by this, and so I asked her what she knew, but she just said, 'We don't really know anything love'. I nodded my head and my eyes welled up with tears again, and they both squeezed my hands and said to me, 'You know, we often told Mum not to trust John as much as she did'. It was then that I told them, without going into too much detail, the 'basics' of what John had done to me.

It was two hours later that I went to bed, where Michael was by now fast asleep and oblivious to the long conversation that I'd had with my sisters that night. As I lay in bed listening to Michael snoring, the familiar emotions of betrayal played on my mind, as I had told yet more people of the secret that I was going to take to my grave with me.

Chapter 34

THE FUTURE

Four years on, and I finally felt able to set into motion the task of finding out how to obtain the court transcripts from 1959. I was not well off enough, financially to employ a solicitor to do the work for me, and I didn't really know where to start. I thought that perhaps the logical thing for me to do first would be to phone the Victoria Law courts, which was the official name for the Birmingham High court, and ask someone in the records office for any information. When I explained to the person on the other end of the 'phone exactly what I was after, she said that she needed to speak to someone in higher authority, and that if I left my phone number, she would get back to me as soon as possible.

I anxiously awaited her return call, and when it came, I was grateful for her help as it held out some hope of me getting the information that I was after. She told me that the transcripts were no longer held in Birmingham, but she did give me a London telephone number, and told me that court transcripts of that age should be held there. I felt full of hope now, as it meant that I would at last be able to see for myself exactly what had been said at the trial. It would enable me at last to learn how it was possible for two people to get away with manslaughter, and another for perjury, never mind 'accidental death'. I never did suppose for a moment that any one of them set out to take a child's life that day, but at least one of them could have had the compassion to speak up that day in the courtroom, it might just have saved me from all that was to follow me throughout my life.

By this time I had finished taking the call it was late afternoon, so I decided not to telephone the London number until the following day. When I 'phoned the number given to me, a lady answered the phone, to whom I explained that I had been given this number by Birmingham Law court, as I needed to get hold of a court transcript from 1959. I fully expected her to ask for the details, and I imagined her writing down dates, names

Lollipops, Bubblegum, Death and Lies

and places, and for her to then say 'I'll get back to you'. But no, you can imagine how I felt when she simply informed me that any court transcripts from 1959 would have been destroyed by now!. My eyes once again filled with tears as I thanked her for her time, but as I put the phone back into it's cradle, I felt that I had been dealt yet another blow. Those records would have shown that it involved a death, that I was personally involved, and as I was still alive, surely I had every right to see what had been said that day. This latest news had destroyed the only hope I had left to try and start burying the past, as now I would never know what had been said on oath by the likes of John Hathaway, or these other people, Ward, and Woodford. I was hurting all over again now, and I felt that the Justice that could have been mine, by at least knowing the truth, had just been snatched away from me.

After yet more tears, the anger and confusion returned, as I wanted those past events closed, and now I knew that they could never be. I felt so let down, and the familiar, nagging question of 'why?' returned to my mind once again. I knew that if I had received some answers, it would perhaps have explained why Fred had always held me responsible for Susan's death. It would also have answered some of the questions that Pamela wanted the ask, because as she had told me herself, that that day was a blank to her. Yes, she remembers some of the day, but as she had said, was that because she had heard talk of it over the years, rather than it be her own remembrances of the day?. On the break up of Elwyne and Fred's marriage, Pam was only 15 years old, and like many teenagers torn with a love for both parents, she would stay with Elwyne one week, then with Fred on another. She has told me numerous times, that when Fred was drunk, he would cry for Susan, and then look at Pamela and ask her, 'why couldn't it have been you?'!!.

On one occasion, Jane asked me if I had tried to obtain a Coroners court transcript. So after the session, I came home and straight away tapped into the internet for the telephone number of the Birmingham Coroners Office. I phoned the number without much hope, but anything would be better than just leaving it there. I spoke to a lovely woman and explained what I was looking for, and why. She asked me to write a letter for her attention, with all of the details of the accident, date, names, area, etc., and that

Lollipops, Bubblegum, Death and Lies

she would enter the city archives and let me know if anything was there. I was lucky, the returning letter informed me that she had found the transcripts, and if I wanted them (did I just!) she required a fee for £16.50, and once that had been received, she would retrieve the transcripts and send them onto me. True to her word, and not having to wait too many days, the envelope dropped on the carpet, so I literally dropped everything and tore open the envelope. The very first thing I read made my eyes blur over and I could not stop the tears from falling but I continued to read. I was never aware of exactly what had contributed to Susan's death, and now I was looking at the cause,......'Shock, due to multiple injuries, including a ruptured lung, spleen, and liver, and a fractured pelvis',....why dear God, could you not have made her death instant, that poor child, my niece, my innocent niece, had no idea what was happening to her, and reading the report broke my heart. No wonder, to my recollection, there wasn't much blood, I was right about the internal injuries. Susan had died at 3 pm, and as if her death was not tragic enough, a post mortem had to be performed on that still, lifeless little body.

The other details in the Coroners Court

transcripts confirmed much of what I remembered, and what some of what the newspaper cuttings had revealed, but I was surprised by the number of witness statements that said they thought it was Woodford, and not Ward who was driving the lorry. I was also amazed at the way that Ward had made his statement, in which he said to the police that he had been told by My Dad, my Mum, and <u>ME</u> that it wasn't his lorry!. I have never in my life spoken to Bob Ward, let alone at the time of the accident!. The police do seem to have made efforts to establish the facts, about who was driving the lorry, and to basic forensic examinations, etc., but the Coroners verdict only draws the conclusion of **'Death by Misadventure'**, and **'by the Bedford lorry reg. TOG 180, being driven by a driver who on the available evidence is not known'**.

It would seem then, that anything further in the way of prosecution by the police would have been dealt with at the Victoria (Birmingham) Law Courts on a later date, and without obtaining those transcripts as well, we will never know of the end result.

It has been an long road for me to trek and sometimes I did feel, 'what's the point in carrying on seeing Jane?', nothing is working, it isn't going to take the past away, nor is it going to bring Susan back. It was never going to make me forget the abuse I was subjected to, and I was never going to hold that precious little baby that I had given birth to and ultimately lost. I would break my heart on each visit to see her, and sometimes I could barely talk it was so painful. So what was the point?.

As I have already said, I know that I have come a long way, and perhaps I do have to accept, that what lies in the past is best left there. I can now talk openly and honestly about my life to anyone who is willing to listen, and I no longer burst into tears at the very thought of the past anymore. The fact that I was a child, (size doesn't come into it),when all of this happened, meant that I had no idea how to express my feelings, but having reached my adult years the time became right for me to 'let go'. However, I still blame myself for Susan's death, but then, that is my prerogative.

Jane once suggested that I might write a letter to Susan, as a kind of therapy, and to write down all the things that I would like to say to her now, but I did not write that letter to her until the 10th August 2005, as somehow I felt that it was the right date, if not the right year, to write it, and even then, as I was writing it out, tears flowed freely from me and plopped onto the card.

When Ginnette was visiting me one day, I told her what Jane had suggested, that I had followed her advice through, and had written a card for Susan. Ginnette asked me if she could take the card with her to read in her own house, and so I allowed her to take it away for a couple of days.

On the front of the card was a picture of a teddy bear, sitting under a table laden with cakes and jelly, and streamers adorning the open table cloth, with the words **'Make a wish'**. Inside the card I had written as follows:

Dear Susan,

Well my love, you are now 51 years old!, but my, it's been 45 years since we have seen each other, you were only an innocent 5 year old when I last saw you, with your beautiful long blonde wavy hair, and your sweet face.

How have things been for you?. I understand that you are now back with your Mum and Dad. I hope that you are happy, you at least deserve that.

Have you seen Nanny and Grandad, if so will you please pass on my love and give them a big hug. Can you tell them that they now have four great grandchildren. Bethen, Jordan, Lucy and Millie.

I must ask you, are there lots of flowers and trees where you are, and is it peaceful?, I do hope so. I have one last thing to ask of you, well two really.

1) Forgive me............Please!

2) If there is a baby girl up there looking for her Mummy and Daddy, tell her that there is a Mummy and Daddy here on earth that love and miss her very much.

Well Susan, I'll say Goodbye for now. I Love and miss you all so much.

God Bless and keep you all safe.

Kisses for Elwyne (your mum)xxxxxxxx I never meant to hurt her or take you away from her. XXXXX

When Ginnette returned the card to me, she told me that she had put something inside the card, but that I could take it out again if I wanted to. When I opened the card, Ginnette had placed a single pressed, dried rose inside. It was a wonderfully simple gesture, and I was touched by the thought that she had done that.

I told Jane that I had written a card out for

Susan, and she asked me what I was going to do with it now that I had written it?. When I asked her what she meant, she told me that by burying or burning the card, I would be letting go of the past. There is still something that is holding me back from letting go, but I am becoming stronger, and I am now feeling optimistic that day will soon come.

For now I still have that card in my possession,...... **Maybe one day I will let go.**

END

Lightning Source UK Ltd.
Milton Keynes UK
178002UK00001B/5/P